DATE DUE

12-17-05	

GAYLORD   PRINTED IN U.S.A.

THUNDER OF
THE CAPTAINS:
The Short Summer
in 1950

DAVID DETZER

THUNDER

OF THE

CAPTAINS

The Short Summer
in 1950

Thomas Y. Crowell Company
Established 1834   New York

Copyright © 1977 by David Detzer

All rights reserved. Except for use in a review, the reproduction or utilization of this work in any form or by any electronic, mechanical, or other means, now known or hereafter invented, including xerography, photocopying, and recording, and in any information storage and retrieval system is forbidden without the written permission of the publisher. Published simultaneously in Canada by Fitzhenry & Whiteside Limited, Toronto.

Manufactured in the United States of America

Library of Congress Cataloging in Publication Data
Detzer, David.
    Thunder of the Captains: The Short Summer in 1950
    Bibliography: p.
    Includes index.
    1.   Korean War, 1950–1953.   I.   Title.
DS918.D45   951.9'042   76-25472
ISBN 0-690-01202-0

1   2   3   4   5   6   7   8   9   10

For Christopher, for Curtis, for Katrina—
with love

Acknowledgments

I want to thank the hundreds of people who helped me in so many ways, and I only wish that somehow I could blame them for whatever flaws this book contains. Unfortunately I must take sole responsibility. I would particularly like to thank the following for their aid: Albert D. Biderman, Carroll Blanchard, Colonel Philip S. Day, Colonel John Doody, George Elsey, Gabriel Kolko, Walter LaFeber, Chong-sik Lee, Betty Boyers Mathews, Merle Miller, Glenn D. Paige, Dean Rusk, and Brigadier General Charles B. Smith (Ret.). Librarians, especially those concerned with research, are indeed a special breed of people. I want to express my appreciation to the library staffs at Carlisle Barracks, Columbia University, the Department of State, the Douglas MacArthur Memorial, the Dwight D. Eisenhower Library, the George Arents Research Library (Syracuse University), the George C. Marshall Library, the Harry S. Truman Library, the Joint University Libraries (Nashville), the Lyndon Baines Johnson Library, the Minnesota Historical Society, the National Archives, the Nebraska State Historical Society, the Ohio Historical Society, Princeton University, the State Historical Society of Wisconsin, Sterling Library (Yale), the University of Connecticut, and Western Connecticut State College.

I am particularly grateful to Garrett Lyke, Edward Peritz, and Robert Noyes for their friendship and enthusiasm; to the Council on East Asian Studies and the Harry S. Truman Library for their grants; and to Ludwell and Dorothy Denny for their encouragement.

Preface

This is a narrative of two weeks in 1950. It is a tale of some men who gave orders and others who followed them. It is about officials in Washington, in Tokyo, in London and Paris and Moscow and Seoul, about diplomats in New York and young soldiers in Asia. It is also, in a small way, an informal portrait of the American nation at midcentury. It is, most of all, about people.

On June 25, 1950, a civil war began in Korea. The two sides, North and South, were divided by conflicting social and economic patterns and by the personal ambitions and fears of their leaders. The United States was under little obligation to enter the conflict. It had no formal alliance with the Republic of Korea in the South. But within a week Harry S. Truman decided to commit America's forces to Korea.

This book is about that decision. It tells how Truman and a handful of his advisers, acting in secret sessions, moved the country into war. It explores some of the immediate results of that decision, including a description of the first American battle there.

During that short summer of 1950 politicians in Washington and soldiers in Korea became melded together. This is their story.

Contents

... And he smelleth the battle afar off, the thunder of the captains, and the shouting.

—Job 39:25

PART ONE: TO WAR

"Welcome to Videoland, Boys and Girls"

Once in a while you find yourself in an odd situation. You get into it by degrees and in the most natural way but, when you are right in the midst of it, you are suddenly astonished and ask yourself how in the world it all came about.

—Thor Heyerdahl, *Kon-Tiki*
(1950)

HARRY S. TRUMAN FELT hot and sticky. His double-breasted suit crumpled into forlorn wrinkles, his shirt collar ran with sweat. Washington heat was undulating from the sidewalks when, about an hour before noon, Truman settled into his seat on the *Independence*, the presidential plane, for the short flight to Baltimore's new Friendship International airport. The president alighted briefly and performed his traditional function as America's head cheerleader. "I dedicate this airport," he told the crowd, "to the cause of peace in the world." Amidst perfunctory clapping he retreated to his plane for the 950-mile flight to Kansas City. This weekend was planned as a presidential vacation.

Events in the world, while itchy with international tensions, seemed less ominous than usual. During the previous week the CIA had reported several potential problem areas but nothing immediately serious: some troop movements in Bulgaria along the Yugoslav border; a few expected difficulties in Berlin; the ebb and flow of guerrilla warfare in Indochina and in the Philippines; and another rumor of a possible flare-up in Korea. It appeared an opportune time to leave soggy Washington for a few days in Independence, Missouri. Some private matters, involving the family farm run by Truman's brother Vivian, needed tending. Besides, Harry missed his wife, Bess, and their only child, Margaret, who were staying in Missouri at the moment.

The Trumans were amazingly close. The three of them liked to do almost everything together—eat, play cards, talk. Members of the White House staff sometimes chuckled affectionately and called them "The Three Musketeers." According to pollsters, many Americans despised Truman and his government, but almost everyone had to admit their president was a good family man. The most casual newspaper reader knew a dozen stories about what magazines were wont to call The First Family. Like the time Harry visited his ninety-two-year-old mother, Martha Truman, in the hospital. She was a tough, unreconstructed Confederate Missourian. She had tripped and broken her hip and shoulder, and was all bandaged when her worried son visited her bedside. He smiled down on her, but before he could utter a word she snapped, "I don't want any smart cracks out of you. I saw your picture in the paper last week putting a wreath at the Lincoln Memorial."[1] Another story involved a letter Truman wrote a music reviewer who suggested Margaret's operatic voice might stand improvement. The president, troubled by the death of a good friend, threatened the reviewer with such general mayhem that he might need beefsteak for his eyes "and a supporter below."

Most presidents have not publicly talked that straight. They have primly posed for posterity and carefully covered up all their seams. They have normally been staid men, and their history is a bland sea of presidential monotony. Reading about such leaders as William Henry Harrison or even Woodrow Wilson is often a kind of torture, like a long conversation with a very dull but talkative Methodist aunt. Harry Truman was different. While he lacked the depth and character of Washington or Jefferson; while he was neither as heroic as Jackson, nor as poignant as Lincoln, nor as charming as Franklin Delano Roosevelt, nor as witty as Kennedy; while he was not as earthy as Lyndon Johnson, or as neurotic as Nixon, he was, in his own way, interesting—probably because he seemed to be "typical."

He always wore a suit, a white shirt, and a tie. Even on the most informal Washington occasions he never removed his coat. He only dressed casually on vacations away from the capital, when he sported garish and rather silly Hawaiian shirts. His most appealing trait was his unpretentious simplicity. Probably no other president ever discontinued conversations with kings or ministers to introduce them to a butler or usher who had just entered the room.[2]

He even had the strength of character to admit his own humiliations. Once, after he left office, he spoke to some students taking a tour of the Truman Library in Independence. A small boy in the auditorium raised his hand and asked, "Mr. President, was you popular when you was a boy?"

"Why, no," Truman answered. "I was never popular. The popular boys were the ones who were good at games and had big tight fists. I was never like that. Without my glasses I was blind as a bat, and to tell the truth, I was kind of a sissy. If there was any danger of getting into a fight, I always ran." Perhaps he had this weakness in mind when at age fifteen he abruptly quit practicing the piano. "I decided it was sissy," he said.[3] We cannot know how much of his

later toughness, and even his flashes of opinionated mean-
ness, were compensations for his early insecurities. Or how
much of his celebrated barnyard vocabulary was an attempt
to be "un-sissy."

Some of the most appealing Truman stories involve his
direct crudity. There was the time Bess Truman held a
party for some ladies in the Rose Garden. Harry came out,
apparently to visit Bess, saw the women there, and turned
bashful and awkward. He stared over the ladies' heads,
obviously trying to think of some light chatter, something
clever to say. At last he blurted out, "Bess, I think the roses
need some more manure," and he spun on his heel and fled.
An awkward pause followed. Then one of the women
turned to the First Lady and confided, "Really, Mrs. Truman, you should train your husband to say 'fertilizer,' not
'manure.'" Bess shook her head wryly and said, "Dear, do
you realize how long it took me to get him to say manure?"4

A similar tale involved Truman's eightieth birthday party.
Years after he had left the White House and become a
rather beloved father figure, some politicians from Kansas
City decided to give him a party. It was to be a rather fancy
afternoon affair in the ballroom of one of the local hotels.
Harry arrived promptly at one o'clock and vigorously waved
his cane hello at the reception committee awaiting him at
the entranceway. They straightened their ties while their
spokesman, one of Missouri's dumber congressmen, stepped
forward.

"Mr. President," he said, "welcome and happy birthday.
We have a room and bath for you to retire to before we go
into the party."

"Bath?" said Harry. "What the hell do I want with a
bath? I already took a piss before I started."

And he sauntered into the hotel.5

On other occasions Truman could be cold and tough; his
blue eyes could glint like frosty steel. During his presidency
in the years just after World War II, his petty, small-town

suspicions of Kremlin Reds and occasional tendencies toward patriotic pugnacity were not only unstatesmanlike but
unfortunately tended to reinforce Stalin's own petty, small-
town suspicions. Certainly Truman must bear at least part
of the blame for the cold war. He knew the Soviet Union
was no immediate threat to either the United States or
Western Europe. The United States was incomparably the
most powerful nation in the world. The fact that he and his
secretaries of state (especially Dean Acheson) chose to feign
shock at supposed Russian bellicosity only indicated that the
president was not above occasional diplomatic sham. His
virginal squeals of surprise at Russian "intransigence" were
mere posturings, meant to persuade Americans in general
and Congress in particular to support his administration's
policies—including various foreign aid bills and military ex-
penditure packages.

The United States of Harry Truman is impossible to describe accurately. Any discussion of its people or history is
only a fragment of reality. A great nation is a mosaic, molded
from an infinite variety of many-colored parts. The United
States in 1950 was fantastically complicated: It was a
classless society with dozens of subtle and important
socioeconomic gradations; it was a democracy in which a
large percentage of the adult population was prevented from
voting by carefully designed racial restrictions; it was a free
society which locked masses of its citizens—including many
of its women—into predetermined patterns of drudgery and
failure and despair. It had a glorious tradition of broad-
based education, but it paid its teachers abysmal salaries
and gave them a status somewhat below successful car
salesmen. Its painters, novelists, architects, sculptors, and
playwrights were among the most vital craftsmen in the
world, yet Americans remained self-conscious about their
culture. Many sneered at their intellectuals, who in turn
sneered back at America's vulgarity and its "booboisie." Its

intellectuals derided their country as a cultural wasteland and whipped themselves into artistic frenzies over their own failure to be born French.

The Bureau of the Census that year calculated that the center of America's population was somewhere in south-central Illinois. If you found that spot, stood on it, and spun slowly around, you could see backward and forward a hundred years. The nation was both very old and very new. It still had more than 75,000 one-room schoolhouses, but it had come a long way. In 1935 only one-tenth of America's farms were electrified; in 1950 about seven out of eight had electricity. A British productivity team visiting the United States discovered that the small one-family farm was becoming almost entirely automated. [6]

A little boy named Kenny Young, aged ten, lived in Oklahoma. During the summer of 1950 Kenny's parents proudly installed their first indoor bathroom. Not everyone in Oklahoma, however, was atuned to modern plumbing. Before the boy's uncle came to visit, his mother carefully instructed him to display the family's new room. After dinner Uncle Jim announced that he figured he'd better step outside for a spell. Kenny, as he still remembers, solemnly rose to do his duty. "Let me show you where our new bathroom is, Uncle Jim," he said. "Look, son," the older man replied sternly, offering the boy an important lesson about life and social relationships, "you don't shit in my house, and I won't shit in yours." [7]

The postwar boom in housing continued. Near (or just beyond) the city limits of most of the country's metropolitan centers sprang tacky clusters of instant suburbs. Near Chicago and Philadelphia, near Los Angeles and Boston, grew towns of concrete, of rows of boxlike dwellings. The houses were laid out shoulder to shoulder in unimaginative flat rows; each had a tiny handerchief lawn. Most Americans had longed for their own little house: A home was part of the national dream. These new communities, inexpensive replicas of the classier suburban developments of the 1920s, offered status. ("We live on Cedar Drive"—or "Twixt Hills"—or "Squirrel Lane.") A house in the suburbs set you off from the urban crush, gave you a touch of elegance. You had all the conveniences of the city, yet you lived in the "country." Moreover, the process was easy. Ex-GIs did not even have to put down the normal 5 percent, and only paid $56 a month. Some of these new residential centers plunged rapidly into flaky slumdom; others grew increasingly attractive and tasteful as their owners added bushes and flowers and personal touches.

One of the latter was Levittown, Long Island. Bill Levitt, its chief promoter, was a loud and flamboyant wheeler-dealer, the epitome of American grossness. But he built good houses for good prices. They may have looked like Cracker Jack boxes, and esthetes may have termed them unspeakable, but for $7,990 they came with a living room picture window, a fireplace that worked, a kitchen with all the basic appliances, two bedrooms on the first floor with more possible upstairs, and a built-in Admiral TV. Levittown offered parks and playgrounds, three huge swimming pools, baseball diamonds, shopping centers, and more than sixty fraternal clubs and veterans' organizations. For $7,990 residents lived in an area previously only populated by potato farmers and characters out of F. Scott Fitzgerald. No wonder 40,000 people moved there in the first three years, most of them incredibly young. Of Levittown's 8,000 children, only a little over 10 percent were more than seven years old. At last America had gotten rid of its embarrassing old people.

For better or worse, Levittown was a strong contender for being The Future.

Americans categorized themselves by incredibly subtle processes. Despite the efforts of journalists and politicians to generalize in convenient generic packages, there was no such thing as the "American people." Vermont Yankees, Sioux Indians, Polish-American coal miners, Alabama Klansmen, Puerto Rican housewives, Rockefeller debutantes—the only classification they had in common was that they lived within the confines of the United States. Each was almost totally ignorant of the others. Each lived in isolated archipelagoes. The nation was fissured by interlaced groupings of age and income, profession and ethnic background, education, sex, and geographic patois. Communities were divided by tastes in clothing, automobiles, and hair styles.

Americans were filled with prejudices. In California a gentleman named Sei Sei Fuji could not acquire clear title to his land because a local ordinance prevented Japanese from owning land. In East St. Louis, Illinois—despite contrary state legislation going back to 1880—schools were still segregated by Jim Crow *laws.*

Six barbers in the government community of Los Alamos, New Mexico, quit their jobs rather than clip the hair of a black security inspector. The barbershop's manager advertised throughout the state for replacements and interviewed twenty-nine candidates, but could find no one who would take the job. For several months males in Los Alamos had to drive thirty-four miles to Santa Fe to get their haircuts.

None of this was new. The United States had always had its bigots. What was most interesting about this period was that editors began to consider these incidents newsworthy—and they were, because in each case they indicated a change. Mr. Fuji's predicament was hardly unique; that he won his court case was unusual. Jim Crow laws in Illinois are not surprising; the fact that they were eradicated that year was a small step ahead. Inspector William Stone's difficulties in Los Alamos were not extraordinary; that he retained his position while the barbers were let go was newsworthy.

Compared to a later age the country reeked with racism, but examined against its own past the United States was making important, if undramatic, strides.

During the summer of 1950 a survey of southern newspapers revealed that many journals in the border area were less condescending toward blacks than they had been. A few papers started to use the designations "Mr." and Mrs." Others hired black reporters; a few even carried regular columns by blacks. [8]

In Pell City, Alabama, a white thug received five years in the penitentiary for manslaughter. He and four others had been charged in the night-riding murder of a black man. The release of the other four and the relatively small sentence were not as significant as the conviction: It may well have been the first case in modern times in which a white man was convicted by a white Alabama jury for murdering a black.

Jim Crow regulations were under attack and barriers were falling everywhere. Presbyterians that year desegregated their mountain resort in Montreat, North Carolina. The American Bowling Congress, the last American sports organization with a "white males only" clause in its constitution, voted to erase it. Bowlers had not changed: They were the same beer-and-sweat men they had always been. The difference was that they felt the pressure of four separate lawsuits and injunctions.

America's judicial system, as creaky and unfair as it often seemed, turned the corner on civil rights that summer. For almost four decades NAACP lawyers had attacked Jim Crow. Nineteen fifty was the year a haphazard trickle turned into a deluge. Although later generations would celebrate the famous 1954 decision of *Brown* v. *Board of Education,* they would often forget that the foundation had been laid by years of patient legal work. During a period of one month in 1950 the Supreme Court outlawed segregation on interstate railroad dining cars, ordered the University of Texas law school to accept a particular black applicant, told the University of Oklahoma to stop segregating its lone black graduate student, and demanded that the University of Missouri accept three black applicants.

The NAACP was not satisfied. In late June it held a conference. Thurgood Marshall, director of its legal department, announced, "We are going to insist on nonsegregation in American public education from top to bottom— from law school to kindergarten."[9] No trumpets blared, but in a sense perhaps a revolution had just been announced.

The year had the usual quota of crimes. Statistics indicated a gradual increase in murder, robbery, and rape; juvenile delinquency rose again after several declining years.

On January 17, 1950, seven men committed the year's most dramatic single crime when they held up Brink's, Incorporated, and carried away more than $2,500,000.

During the year Senator J. William Fulbright investigated connections between certain governmental agencies and what newspapers solemnly called "The Underworld." Eventually these investigations revealed considerable corruption in both the Internal Revenue Service and the Reconstruction Finance Corporation. The RFC, created by Herbert Hoover in the early thirties to combat the depression, had become a soft touch for faltering companies with the proper Washington connections. Fulbright announced that the RFC had loaned a Reno gambling casino, with "close connections to the underworld," a million dollars.[10] Harry Truman was furious with Fulbright for "attacking his administration." The president called the Arkansas politician "Senator Halfbright."

Another senatorial inquiry delved into organized crime. Estes Kefauver, senator from Tennessee, bright and extremely ambitious, introduced America to the sinister world of racketeers and murder. Few indictments resulted from the revelations but many citizens did become aware of the problem. The following exchange took place at one of the hearings.

"Do you know what the Mafia is?"

"What?"

"The Mafia. M-a-f-i-a?"

"I am sorry. I don't know what you are talking about."[11]

A fascinatingly repugnant reptile named Frank Costello was Kefauver's greatest find. Costello had a round, surly face and spoke with such broken syntax that he achieved self-caricature, a Hollywood gangster spewing lies and venom from the side of his mouth. His lawyers refused to allow their client to be televised directly, so in one of television's first coups the camera followed Costello's fingers. An enraptured home audience watched the hoodlum's knuckles twist nervously back and forth as he declared the absolute innocence of those hands. Cinéma vérité at its best.

In 1950 the Coca-Cola Company made a net profit of $38 million, a third of which derived from overseas income. *Time* reported that some French officials had become so concerned at the soda pop threat to their wine industry they were attempting to ban Coke from their shores. (Consider the implications: scar-faced rings of Mafiosi smuggling secret caches of illicit soft drinks into Marseilles, and the shuttered doors of glossy bistros where one could purchase bathtub cola.) Egyptians drank 350 million Cokes a year; one vendor displayed his red Coca-Cola sign within a hundred yards of the pyramids. *In hoc signo vinces.*[12]

In 1950 Camels cigarettes advertised, "Not one single case of throat irritation due to smoking Camels."

The prices of most items at that time seem low to a later, nostalgic generation, but quality was also generally low. And wages for most people began at seventy-five cents an hour.

Canasta was the rage. Enthusiasts formed clubs of fellow fanatics. Newspapers ran canasta columns which supplied advice on the game's finer points.

A thirty-two-year-old evangelist named Billy Graham spoke to growing throngs. Religious observance—and maybe even devotion—was staging a comeback. Yet, according to the Commerce Department, the nation spent twenty times as much on clothing accessories and jewelry as on religion and social welfare combined; it spent two and a half times as much on liquor as it did on medical care; it spent three times as much on tobacco as on both private education and all types of research.

Among the year's titillating news items were the frilly panties of pretty tennis player Gussie Moran and the warm friendship between Italian director Roberto Rossellini and Ingrid Bergman. The Swedish movie star made headlines when she admitted that the source of her pregnancy was not her doctor-husband but Rossellini. Many Americans expressed shock; for years afterward some parents refused to allow their daughters to see any Bergman movies. To prevent the Bergman scandal from setting off a congressional investigation of Hollywood's morals, Ronald Reagan, president of the Screen Actors Guild, declared that "Hollywood is pretty much a goes-to-bed-with-the-chickens town."[13]

It was the year that Liz Taylor married (and left) Nickie Hilton, that Shirley Temple, aged twenty-two, married Charles Black, and that fifty-six-year-old Cary Grant wed Betsy Drake and eloped in a plane piloted by best man Howard Hughes.

Americans had opinions about all kinds of things. A majority thought most profits ended up in "the pockets of the big bankers and financiers in Wall Street." Most gentlemen preferred brunettes, and surprisingly enough almost half the country's males who were asked said they would vote for a woman president. (Slightly more than half the females said they would do the same.) A third of those polled declared they would support a Prohibition law. Most people believed that spiritual values and personal happiness were going downhill. Yet 53 percent could not name even *one* of the four Gospels.[14]

Anti-communism flavored the political discussions. On June 24, 1950, the *New York Times* featured the following articles on its first five pages:

California U. Ousts Anti-Red Oath Foes
(Regents Discharge 157 of Staff Who Failed to Sign Statement)

Hearing Deferred in Espionage Case

81 Files on Loyalty Held Inconclusive
(Lodge Calls Data from State Department "Unfinished")

Government Argues That "Intent" Convicts the Communist Leaders

Judge Acts Thursday on 3 of "Hollywood 10"

Negro Association [NAACP], After Stormy Debate, Orders Heads to "Eradicate" Red Influence

Africa Negro Riots Assessed in Study
(Investigation of Events in the Johannesburg Area Finds Reds Active Among the Natives)

Bulgarian Threats to Yugoslavia in Armed "Provocations" Alleged

Anti-Red Front Urged

Soviet Hints Action on Berlin Barge Ban

Red Paper in Guatemala

Virulent anti-radicalism, common in the United States for decades, was accelerated by Truman's loyalty program of 1947. The president himself had indicated Communists might have infiltrated American society, and anti-"communism" spread across the country, touching hamlets, cities, industries, schools, unions. Part of it was a fad: An association of amateur archers in California voted to require loyalty oaths for membership. Part of it was much more malignant. The demand for "servile patriotism" went deeper than anti-radicalism. According to polls only 3 per-

cent of Americans considered communism "the most important problem the U.S. Government must solve in the next
year [1950]." Only 58 percent could provide a reasonable
definition for the term "cold war."[15] Probably much of
"McCarthyism" consisted of attacks on things and people
and ideas which local groups opposed—for example, foreign
cars or Ivy League education. Harry Truman (and later,
Senator Joe McCarthy) legitimated demands for conformity
and generalized assaults on pet peeves: The label "Communist" became a convenient excuse.

The year was not especially distinguished for its music;
much of it seemed written by high school students majoring
in music depreciation.

Plays on Broadway offered variety and remarkable quality. A list of them, for the day the Korean War began, looked
like this:

> Come Back, Little Sheba
> Death of a Salesman
> Detective Story
> Gentlemen Prefer Blondes
> Julius Caesar
> Kiss Me, Kate
> Lost in the Stars
> Peep Show
> Mister Roberts
> Peter Pan
> South Pacific
> Texas, Li'l Darlin'
> The Cocktail Party
> The Consul
> The Happy Time
> The Madwoman of Chaillot
> The Member of the Wedding
> The Wisteria Trees
> Tickets, Please!
> Where's Charley?

That evening's radio shows included the following:

5:00	The Shadow
5:30	True Detective Mysteries
6:00	Roy Rogers Show My Favorite Husband (with Lucille Ball)
6:30	Nick Carter Steve Allen Show
7:00	Guy Lombardo
7:30	The Saint (with Vincent Price) Hit the Jackpot (with Bill Cullen)
8:00	Adventures of Sam Spade Stop the Music (with Bert Parks)
8:30	NBC Symphony Orchestra Red Skelton
9:00	Walter Winchell Meet Corliss Archer
9:30	John Steele, Adventurer Social Democratic Forum (Women in Industry and Politics)
10:00	Take It or Leave It (with Jack Parr)

Television. The small screen emerged from its chrysalis that year. On June 24 a polling agency announced that for the first time a majority of Americans had seen some type of program on TV.[16]

Analysts attempted to calculate the impact of this new phenomenon. *Time* magazine, with its ear pressed to the heart of Middle America, gleefully reported various observations. Sales of raw popcorn had leaped 500 percent. Apparently, innumerable viewers correlated television with the movies. If they munched popcorn in their neighborhood theaters, they gobbled it at home. A professor at Pennsylvania's State College of Optometry worried about eyestrain. He suggested that after a full evening of television, viewers should sit for at least twenty minutes in a darkened room to let their eyes recoup their night vision. An educator in Stamford, Connecticut, became concerned about the climbing rate of academic failures at Burdick Junior High. After taking a survey, Principal Joseph H. Franchina concluded that at least half his students spent as much time in front of the TV as they did in the classroom. Principal Franchina was aghast.[17]

In 1950 television was a magic screen which instantly revealed America's voracious appetite for mediocrity. Variety shows, emceed by Garry Moore, Ed Wynn, Milton Berle, Ed Sullivan, and Arthur Godfrey, continued to be among the most common entertainments. Sports shows included baseball, wrestling, and roller derbies. Big Ten college football barred television from producing their games on the grounds that it would reduce attendance. One of the country's most popular programs was "Kukla, Fran, and Ollie"—an unpretentious puppet show with quiet humor. For some curious reason several million Americans spent each weekday evening entranced by the antics of Fletcher Rabbit, Beulah Witch, Clara Coo Coo, and of course Kukla and Fran and Ollie.

Westerns had not yet become a television staple. (That would come later with the advent of "adult," more sophisticated, themes.) In 1950 Western programs fell in the category of "Six Gun Playhouse"—extensions of Saturday matinee cowboy heroes: gun-toting, clean-living Gene Autry–Roy Rogers–Hopalong Cassidy. Most of all, Hopalong Cassidy.

In 1915 William Boyd ("Hoppy"), born in Ohio, a laborer's son, came to California to search for fame, money, and women. He was a good-looking, husky, devil-may-care, wavy-haired charmer. He first worked as a chauffeur for a rent-a-car agency, met and married a somewhat older Boston heiress, acquired a large, flashy wardrobe, and then divorced her. Cecil B. De Mille saw Boyd and hired him at $30 a week. Soon he was earning $100,000 a year. He became the proverbial Hollywood playboy: yachts, mansions, parties, marriages-and-divorces. In the 1930s he made his first Hopalong Cassidy movie—a simple-minded B western, slotted for the prepubescent trade. Boyd, now platinum-haired and married a fifth time (to a woman he credited with reforming him), eventually made more than sixty Hopalong Cassidy movies.

In the late 1940s Boyd gambled on television. He mortgaged everything and raised $350,000 to acquire full rights to his movies. A Los Angeles station rented one; it proved so popular they tried another. And so it went. During 1950 a Hopalong Cassidy craze erupted. (Media bubbles had existed before, but nothing quite like this. Not even Valentino at his most sultry, or Amos and Andy at their "rib-tickling funniest" had been able to cash in on such a wide variety of paraphernalia.) Children bought millions of Hopalong comic books, Hopalong roller skates (with spurs and genuine glass-jewel-studded ankle straps), Hopalong bicycles (with handlebars shaped like steer horns), Hopalong chaps and boots, hats and shirts, six-shooters and gun belts, as well as Hopalong wallpaper, soap, cookies, candy bars, record albums, and watches. He drew the largest circus attendance in Chicago history.

He was a semiliterate, white-haired, paunchy fifty-five-year-old. His acting ability had been negligible. But Hoppy was a new phenomenon: In an age of Communist spies and atom bombs, he was an apparently unaffected kiddie-hero. He was simplicity. He was a refracted, childhood mirror of Milton Berle, roller derbies, and a clan of marvelous fast-talking hucksters who could fascinate a TV audience for half an hour demonstrating a simple potato slicer.

America was experiencing a delayed final belch of her nineteenth century. Early television presented the last of a disappearing breed of Americana—crude, shallow, and un-sophisticated, redolent of the faint odor of stale cigars and horse manure. Those potato slicer salesmen were pitchmen standing on the backs of their wagons shouting at the crowds. Berle was vaudeville; Hopalong Cassidy was the dime novel. They were all already anachronistic—which was probably the source of part of their popularity; when they faded, a tiny part of American history died.

For a moment during the summer of 1950 the United States stood frozen between the Past and the Future.

Then she tipped.

CHAPTER TWO

The Conquistadors

Great stars have great pride.

—Gloria Swanson, *Sunset Boulevard*
(1950)

DOUGLAS MACARTHUR WAS BALD. There was no getting around it. He allowed his few hairs to grow long and combed them over the top of his head, where they lay limp and lonely on his scalp. To some men baldness is an acceptable part of maturity, but to MacArthur it was an affront—a man destined for greatness should not be troubled with the piddling problems of human frailty. The truth was he was getting old. The backs of his hands showed the brown stains of liver spots, and his body, once ripcord lean, bulged tenderly around his middle. His mind strayed: He repeated himself without being aware of it. Yet, here in 1950, General MacArthur was still one of his country's most remarkable men. His life had been a storybook romance, a chapter or so from the American Dream.

Douglas MacArthur's grandfather was a successful and influential Wisconsin lawyer with political connections, briefly governor of Wisconsin, and for many years a judge in the District of Columbia's highest court. Grandfather

MacArthur was genteel and socially vigorous, an absolutely charming raconteur with a taste for fine things. He had not been in Washington long before he became an integral part of its most fashionable society. The city's richest matrons found his manners and wit essential ingredients of their most successful parties.

Young Douglas knew his grandfather, but was aware of him only as an old man flickering briefly though his childhood. It seems unlikely the old judge had much direct effect upon the lad, but a clan is altered for generations by the success of one of its members, and partly because of Grandfather MacArthur young Douglas was brought up to appreciate his family's respectability and prominence. No doubt some of Douglas's later arrogance grew out of this training.

His father, Arthur MacArthur, was an army officer, a certified war hero who won the Congressional Medal of Honor for bravery during the Civil War. His mother, Mary, was a southern belle, born on her family's mansion along the Elizabeth River in Virginia, and called "Pinky" by her relations. She was a stately, determined woman, absolutely devoted to her son's career. A later generation might consider her pushy and somewhat odd. While her son was at West Point, Pinky lived at one of the nearby hotels so as always to be close to him. She raised him to have immense pride—in his country, in his family, in himself.

Douglas was born in 1880 in an army barracks near Little Rock, Arkansas; he spent most of his childhood on the flat, dusty soil of western military posts. By the time he reached manhood, it was obvious he was something special. A list of his abilities and accomplishments are a catalog of almost every boy's daydreams. He was, for instance, incredibly bright. As a West Point cadet he achieved one of the highest averages ever attained there: 98.14. Douglas was also recognized at the Academy as a leader, chosen First Captain of the Corps, the approximate equivalent of president of the student body. And although skinny as a swagger stick, he pushed himself hard enough to win his varsity letter in baseball. Moreover, he was handsome, with the dark, debonair good looks of an actor: thick brows, a wide mouth with full lips, the regal nose of a hawk. Pictures of him before he turned fifty reveal a man with a zest for life, often with an engaging grin on his face. Throughout his career his physical courage was awesome: He casually performed acts of incredible bravery. He would stand calmly erect while shells detonated and shrapnel flew around him. He seemed oblivious to danger while lesser men ran for cover. Perhaps, when the bullets ricocheted near him, his body shrank in human fear, but if so he never let on. He exuded the supreme self-confidence of a Greek demigod.

Douglas MacArthur, listening to the plucked lyre-strings of his destiny, was a character out of Homer. The army had never had anyone like him. Generals George Patton and Joseph Stilwell and Ulysses S. Grant were fighters; Dwight D. Eisenhower and George C. Marshall were canny administrators; Robert E. Lee had an ounce of common humanity and the poignant sadness of uncertainty; George Washington, the country squire, retained the crude awkward strength of a farmer. Douglas MacArthur seemed different: He was an imperial patrician practicing military life in the grand manner. He appeared meant by the gods to be at least a viceroy.

Although he never admitted it, he did have defects. His sense of humor, if any, was microscopic. His humility was even smaller. Constant striving for perfection made him hypersensitive to any criticism, to the least suggestion that he might have flaws. He surrounded himself with lackeys who assiduously petted his towering ego. Stories were legion of the way he used newspapermen to plump up his prestige.

By 1950 MacArthur's international reputation was based on both his military and political acumen. Yet his superiority in both these areas was vastly overrated. His military abilities, while greater than average, had allowed during his career for serious blunders, several occurring in the first months of World War II. (In the Philippines, for example, he foolishly left his entire air force lined up wing-tip to wing-tip after receiving definite word about the Japanese attack on Pearl Harbor. Most of the planes were still sitting on the ground when the low-flying Japanese force strafed and bombed them into scrap.) Every military leader makes mistakes. MacArthur, however, refused to admit his, and his literary flunkies made careers out of blaming others for his errors.

The saddest part of his character was his overweening governmental ambitions. Despite a political naiveté that bordered on silliness, he hungered for the presidency with all his fiber. In 1944 and again in 1948 he offered himself to the American citizenry. They in their infinite wisdom turned him down.

The most incredible aspect of his life was that it evolved in separate chronological layers like geological formations. During World War I he helped create the famous Rainbow Division and distinguished himself in battle by leading it across the fields of northern France. After the war he became the superintendent of West Point, one of the youngest in its history. Before he arrived there the Academy was basically a technical school, providing archaic knowledge to yawning students. MacArthur brought to the institution his determination to modernize it, to bring it educationally and socially into the twentieth century. Although he failed to make it a major area of academic study, it did become less sterile.

In 1930 he inevitably took his place as the army's chief of staff; he was now the highest-ranking officer in the United States. The next few years were not happy ones for him. Americans traditionally viewed their peacetime soldiers with suspicion and disdain; this period was no exception. The army was not well liked. Nor did MacArthur make it more popular by leading an attack upon several hundred American men, women, and children. The men were veterans of World War I, encamped in Washington to petition Congress. Because of the depression they wanted the government to grant them immediately the few hundred dollars due them for their wartime service. Although Herbert Hoover actually gave the orders to evict this Bonus Army (as the families at Anacostia Flats were called), MacArthur seemed to relish the task too much. (Soon after this, Franklin Delano Roosevelt said he considered MacArthur one of the two most dangerous men in America; Huey Long was the other.)

Later in the thirties MacArthur resigned from the army. The Philippine government had asked him to help train its military. In 1937 he left the United States for Manila; he would not return for fourteen years. The Filipinos held him in awe, idolized him—and he returned their feelings with a warm, if somewhat patronizing, love.

In the early days of World War II his life changed again when Roosevelt chose him to organize and lead the campaign against Japan. Politics played at least some part in the president's decision. MacArthur was a well-known Republican conservative. By placing him on the administration's team, Roosevelt hoped to reduce partisan attacks on the war effort. (Years later Lyndon Johnson, in another context, defined what Roosevelt's philosophy had been: It would be better, as Johnson said about another man, to have MacArthur inside the tent pissing out than outside the tent pissing in.) During the war the general was not always happy. He felt, and rightly so, that the government's chief focus was on Europe. But although Roosevelt's advisers were most concerned about the Nazis, MacArthur was not. He believed, and would continue to believe for the rest of his life, that Asia was more significant than Europe, that Western Europe in particular was decadent, and that the Pacific should become an American lake. He was frustrated by the fact that the European theater received more military forces and the best equipment. He used his large and devoted public relations staff to drum up support for the war against Japan. (Part of his later reputation as an egomaniac resulted from his efforts in these years.) He hoped to get more men and supplies from Washington by increasing his own political wallop, then using it to put pressure on the government. Certainly this was not his only motive for puffing up his reputation—he had done it, at the expense of others, too often throughout his life—but it may have been one of the primary reasons. To help get the kind of military support necessary to defeat Japan, he personalized the war in the Pacific, making himself the center of it. Newspapermen who wanted to cover this theater of the war had to receive his signature, and it was clear they had better glamorize MacArthur's efforts if they wished to retain their official status. (He was once supposed to have said, "I don't care how you write history, gentlemen, as long as it agrees with my communiqués.")

His attempts to force Roosevelt to send him more supplies and men were aided by the political situation in Washington. Republicans could not very well attack the war effort without appearing unpatriotic. On the other hand, not only did some of them genuinely find some aspects of the war unpalatable, but they knew that blanket enthusiasm for Roosevelt's decisions merely aided the Democratic party. They recognized that soon the war would be over; they—along with a few Democratic cohorts, largely from the South, and a number of prominent newspaper and magazine publishers—were looking for some way to dismantle what remained of the New Deal. MacArthur's position in the Pacific was a perfect excuse for them. They could use the general's complaints about his inadequate supplies to attack the administration. MacArthur and this group of high-ranking Republicans used each other for their own purposes, to further their own causes. As a result he became one of the most publicized and politicized generals in

American history. Partly for this reason, Harry Truman chose him after the war to govern Japan: It seemed a simple method of attaining bipartisanship for America's Japanese policies.

No matter what Truman's motives were, the general was a brilliant choice. MacArthur, now an old man, achieved his destiny here in the Land of the Rising Sun—to be a great and kind leader of a devoted people.

Until 1868 Japan had been ruled by a string of military leaders called *shoguns* who ran the country in the name of the emperor. In a sense MacArthur was the last of them. From 1945 until 1951 he remained Japan's benevolent military despot, practicing a sort of participatory autocracy. He dictated their new constitution; he decided who should own land and who should not. He even insisted that Japanese women be allowed to vote. (One day an old Japanese woman threw herself face down on the sidewalk in front of him to show her respect. He picked her up gently and said, "Now, now—we don't do that sort of thing any more." And he patted her shoulder. [1]) All in all he attempted to prescribe a liberal democracy.

He lived in quiet elegance at the American embassy in Tokyo. He rose at seven o'clock. At eight he joined his wife for prayers, Bible reading, and breakfast (two three-minute eggs, toast, and tea). The dining room duplicated America's Federal style: mahogany furniture, round gilt mirrors on the walls, eagles everywhere. Even the servants wore the Great Seal of the United States on their brown kimonos.

After breakfast he retired to another room to read the dispatches which had come in during the night. At ten thirty he left the embassy, climbed into the back of a waiting 1941 black Cadillac, and slowly traveled the ten minutes to his office. As the car, with its five-star insignia on front and back, drove sedately toward Tokyo's major intersections, policemen on duty, watching for him, changed their traffic lights to green. (Never to wait for a red light! Even the saintliest man might be affected by such awesome power.)

Finally he arrived at the Dai Ichi building, a boxlike structure once belonging to an insurance company. At the front entrance two American privates stood tall and immaculate in their khaki uniforms and black lacquered helmets. On the sidewalk a small crowd of Japanese tourists usually milled self-consciously, waiting for their American conqueror to arrive. As he clambered from the Cadillac's back seat, they would bow deeply. And as he strode majestically past, they would turn and snap his picture with their cameras.

His office on the sixth floor was neat and efficient, almost barren. The only personal touch was a table covered with dozens of pipes and a tobacco bowl. No telephone intruded on this sanctuary. He was beyond the mortal reach of Alexander Graham Bell's insistent buzzer. A few pencils and a pad of lined, legal-sized paper were almost the only objects on his desk. He used them throughout the morning to write his letters and speeches.

When he finished his paperwork, he saw whatever visitors he had that day. They had sat perched in his waiting room, a large paneled area with molded doors. (MacArthur, of course, never stooped to visit anyone else—even Emperor Hirohito.)

In the early afternoon he returned to the embassy, where he ate a light lunch, often with a few guests. Afterward he napped for an hour or so. Sometime between four and five he returned to the Dai Ichi building to work into the night with his dedicated aides, most of whom had been with him for years, since the bad days at Corregidor.

His routine almost never varied. He never really saw Japan. In his six years there he only left Tokyo twice—once for the Philippines and once for Seoul, each for short visits. In Japan, moreover, he surrounded himself almost solely with American objects (books, furniture, food) and American people. John Gunther estimated that MacArthur never talked at any length with more than about a dozen Japanese officials, and with them only a handful of times. He never saw *any* Japanese socially. His personal contact with the country would have been almost the same had he stayed in the Waldorf Astoria (where later he would spend his declining years—this time insulating himself from the foreignness of American life). His entire existence in Japan was a *kabuki* drama, a highly stylized and traditional Japanese play in which elaborately costumed actors dance and sing according to meticulously prescribed rites.

Despite his lack of personal contact with Asians, he firmly believed that he understood the "oriental mentality," especially the great emphasis they placed, he thought, on "face," on the mystique of reputation. While there may have been some basis in fact for his dubious hypothesis, only someone of MacArthur's arrogance would have based an entire policy on it. But incredibly enough, it worked. For many years the Japanese accepted American occupation with little complaint. But it is debatable that MacArthur's ukases about democratic principles and practices had half as much effect on Japanese society as he and his journalistic chorus of newspaper supporters thought. Japan is perhaps more, not less, dominated by her plutocracy today than she was in the prewar heyday of the *zaibatsu,* the great economic families of Japan. One can also note that MacArthur himself occasionally suppressed leftist political opponents and their newspapers. Yet, after all such questions and qualifications, the fact remains that MacArthur's tenure in Japan was magnificent—because it could have been much worse. The elements of distrust and hatred were there on both sides in 1945, but remarkably little violence occurred. Certainly the occupation's relative tranquillity was mainly the result of Japanese adaptiveness and good sense, but MacArthur's steadying influence was an important stabilizing factor.

Equally significant in the formation of modern Japan was the American GI. He brought with him his ideals and his swagger, his attitudes and his appetites.

Most GIs gleefully enjoyed their tour of duty in Japan.

One young man told a reporter: "I been shacked up there now with the prettiest moose [girl friend–maid] you ever did see. I got a place to live that beats the dump I lived in for fifteen years at Enid, Oklahoma. I get my meals cooked, my washing done, my socks mended, my orders obeyed like I was MacArthur himself, with no back talk, and all of everything a fellow wants, you know, and it all come to $37 a month. I never had it so good."[2]

Other soldiers hated it. One man there at the time recalled that "lots of guys couldn't adapt themselves. I guess they were just homebodies. Lots of them went off the deep end, Section 8. I had one guy sleeping next to me, crying at night. 'Charlie, what's the matter,' I'd say. And he says, 'I want out. I didn't think it would be like this.' I'd tell him, 'Hell, you only live once, so enjoy it.' But he wouldn't listen."[3]

Later, when American soldiers who had been stationed in Japan lost battles against the North Korean army, journalists and politicians would claim that the problem was that they were pampered Americans, made softer by easy duty in Japan. But such an analysis was not wholly accurate. Much of the military ineptitude they displayed was due to the fact that in Japan they had been "garrison troops," more of a constabulary force than an army. They had volunteered for peacetime service, and all they expected from this duty was to get away from home, to pick up the GI Bill, to have some excitement—"to get a little nookie, you know what I mean?" They were not so much flaccid as they were undertrained and unprepared for war. Just two days before the Korean War began, the military columnist for the *New York Times*, Hanson W. Baldwin, wrote that although the United States had begun to retrain her army a year before, "few if any units are ready for infantry action."[4] As a general named Anthony McAuliffe, commanding an army corps in Japan, said, "This army here is no damn good."[5]

Their native abilities were among the poorest in the entire service. Of the 592,000 soldiers in the American army, the 83,000 in Japan were considered among the least capable. The military bureaucracy in Washington had culled through the army and kept most of the best in the United States or sent them to Europe. The remainder went to Japan. More often than not, these were not America's privileged youth. (Middle-class boys normally knew how to escape the draft, and had good motives for doing so.) These were the children of America's poverty. Their worlds had been ghettos and barrios, farm shacks of warped gray boards, the dingy shadows of coal towns. For them military service was a means to escape the drabness of their home lives, or—at worst—just one more unhappy part of their unhappy existences.

(The American army still recruited men according to their color, despite Harry Truman's famous 1948 order. MacArthur's headquarters in Tokyo, following contemporary army procedure, received replacements in two categories: white and black. According to Eighth Army records, each month its total quota "generally called for 2,520 enlisted white replacements and 270 Negro enlisted replacements."[6] Given America's racist attitudes, black recruits could hardly be considered members of a pampered, flabby generation.)

Perhaps it was their backgrounds, but a large percentage scored abysmally low on IQ tests. Of the enlisted men who first fought in Korea, 43 percent were ranked within the army's two lowest intelligence classifications. In other words *almost half* tested below what the army normally considered *acceptable*.[7]

Even within Japan a sifting process took place. MacArthur's headquarters grabbed the highest-quality recruits; army units near Tokyo took the next highest; those farther out took the next, and so on in concentric rings, farther and farther south. Down near the bottom of Kyushu, the southernmost Japanese island, was the last major military base,

Camp Wood. Stationed here was the central core of the Twenty-fourth Division, the first men to fight in the Korean War.

Camp Wood had once housed a Japanese cavalry outfit. The beautiful red horses were now gone, just a few left, shaggy and bony, pulling "honey wagons"—smelly, sad-looking vehicles carrying loads of human excrement for fertilizer. The camp was pleasant in those last soft days of peace. The region was pretty and warm much of the year, and soldiers in their barracks could sometimes smell the lush aroma of nearby flower blossoms. The base contained most of the comforts of home—and then some. It had movie theaters and barbers and bars. A chaplain named Father Powers tended his flock there; young schoolteachers taught the base's children. Camp Wood even had its own football team, which played others from different posts. And it had a PX which flowed in cornucopian profusion. At tax-free, wholesale prices one could purchase diamonds and booze, cameras and tins of exotic foods. A case of twenty-four bottles of Coca-Cola cost 62¢, a bottle of Scotch was $2.00. One young bride, preparing for married life, bought herself a wardrobe, a Singer sewing machine, a mixmaster, a toaster, an electric roaster, a waffle iron, and a coffee maker. She considered hiring a maid.[8] Servants came admirably cheap: Someone estimated that Americans in Japan employed 25,000 of them.[9]

For those Camp Wood soldiers so inclined, female companionship lay not far away. Kumamoto was just a few miles away; many Americans kept regular girl friends there. Even the principal of the base's school was rumored to have one. Whorehouses in Kumamoto were satisfactorily plentiful, though they were never as varied as in Tokyo, which sported 13 red light districts and perhaps 2,000 licensed houses of prostitution, a few of which contained as many as 500 girls.

The young officers at Camp Wood were a close-knit crew

with a great deal in common. Several were recent West Point graduates. One was Lieutenant Phil Day. He was boyishly handsome and easygoing with a ready smile and a nonchalant attitude toward spit-and-polish. His father had been an army man and Day suffered from the usual insecurities of army brats. (Military children, dragged from base to base, acquire all the roots of a tumbleweed. As a result they are often nail-biters, hungering for security, for genuine friendship. Perhaps MacArthur—another army brat—showed symptoms of this syndrome in his total abhorrence of criticism.) As a teen-ager, up until his third year at West Point, Phil Day had been subtly rebellious. He did not particularly like school in general, or the Academy in particular. In his junior year, however, he began to accept himself and West Point. He even became a cheerleader, encouraging its football eleven to stomp on Navy. But he could never quite force himself to concentrate on academics. Out of his class of 301, he graduated 276th.

In June 1950 Phil Day was married and reasonably settled; his wife was pregnant. He was considering making a career of the army. He seemed in the process of becoming a good officer.

One of Day's West Point classmates had been Jack Doody, now also stationed in Japan. During the early years of World War II he had served in the navy aboard a minesweeper and was therefore older than youngsters like Day— and steadier. During his four years at the Academy he became respected as a leader. But academically he almost scraped the bottom of his class: He ranked 287th out of the 301. By 1950 he was married and had no children.

Phil Day and Jack Doody—and others like them— enjoyed their existence in Japan. Private Burns, for example, eighteen years old, from Stony Island Avenue in Chicago, and Private First Class Florentin Gonzales, a Chicano from the Southwest. There was nineteen-year-old phlegmatic Kenneth Shadrick of Skin Fork, West Virginia, who was about to attain momentary fame as the first American soldier killed in Korea. None of them anticipated the war that was about to engulf them. They remained largely unaware of events a few hundred miles away in Korea, about to draw them away from Camp Wood, about to kill many of them in the ancient bloody ways of battle.

Some were not much more than boys. Their conversations danced with the cryptic phrases of American adolescents. When they went to a bar, they got stoned on whiskey and barfed. Generally they liked to goof off or screw around (or back home, in a stripped-down jalopy, they had bombed around—or gone parking). They chewed gum incessantly. (Bazooka Joe comics, wrapped around pink blocks of bubble gum, defined their humor.) They liked to dance, which meant a fox trot. And you showed how much of a lover you were by grinding your thigh into her groin. (Meanwhile you watched out for guys who might try to cut in and birddog you.) When you got back with your buddies that night they checked your neck for hickies and asked, "Did you go all the way? Did she put out?" Or maybe she was a dog ("Arf, arf") or a dope ("Every party has a pooper, that's why we invited you, Party Pooper"). If you were back in L.A. or a little town in Wisconsin you might have worn a crew cut and saddle shoes; or you might have been a j.d., greased your hair into a d.a., and carried a switchblade. Zoot suits, apparently originated by gangs of Mexican-Americans in Southern California, were now out, but if you wore one and someone else did not like it, it was tuftittie—or, like they say in the Russian marines, toughski-shitski.

And back home your girl, if you had one, might wear a pony tail and maybe your friendship ring, a silver wreath shaped like a victory symbol—which it often was. If she wrote letters to you, she signed them S.W.A.K. and put the stamp upside down on the envelope to indicate her undying devotion. If you did not have a girl, your friends tried to spot your hairy palms.

School was a drag. Only brownies worked hard at it. Teachers were always out to give you the royal shaft.

Ethnic humor was okay. You niggerlipped your cigarettes and jewed down car salesmen—who, you hoped, did not try to jap you back with a lemon.

In 1950 the United States was still an openly racist society and its attitudes infected the country's young soldiers. Next to their lack of proper military training, the most salient feature of America's soldiers in Japan was their ignorant bigotry. Most GIs—black, white, or brown—had a disdain for the average Japanese; and they looked upon Koreans, the niggers of Asia, as totally contemptible. This unfortunate attitude would affect what was about to happen.

CHAPTER THREE

The Year
of the
Tiger

Attack when he is unprepared; sally out when he does not expect you.
—Sun Tzu, *The Art of War*
(c. 400–320 B.C.)

THE ANIMALS HURRIED to Buddha's bedside as he lay dying. The rat arrived first. He rode most of the way on the ox's back, cleverly jumped off at the last moment, and hurried in ahead. The ox lumbered in second. The tiger came third, followed by the rabbit, the dragon, the serpent, and so on. Twelve in all. Each year in an endless cycle is named after one of these twelve beasts: 1950 was The Year of the Tiger.

The Korean peninsula, almost 600 miles long, hangs priapically down from the Asian mainland. Manchuria and the Siberian provinces of the Soviet Union are to the north; Japan is a few hundred miles east. Koreans proudly note they invented a movable-type printing press (50 years before Gutenberg) and an ironclad fighting ship (250 years before the *Monitor* and the *Merrimac*). The average Korean home had central heating when America's Anglo-Saxon progenitors still shivered in thatch huts. Koreans point to their long civilization, older than that of France.

But Korea's position in the geographic cockpit of northeast Asia has made her a battleground for foreign armies.

Near the turn of the twentieth century Japan, Russia, and China fought each other over Korea's prostrate body. In 1905 Japan won the prize. During the next forty years the Japanese modernized Korea's primitive economy, simultaneously squeezing the land of its economic juices. Korea offered coal, iron, gold, and vast quantities of rice to the expanding Japanese Empire. The Japanese ruled her like a penal camp. Their brutal police used secret informers and interrogation by torture. To keep the population under control, Japan denied Koreans their heritage. Korean children could not study their own language in school or their own history.

Then, in August 1945, the Japanese Empire came to an abrupt end. Within a period of three days the United States dropped its atomic bombs on Hiroshima and Nagasaki and Russian divisions hurtled into Manchuria. The Japanese cabinet offered to surrender.

The end came so fast that American policy makers were unprepared; they were unsure what to do now, and they were worried. Although the Japanese government might have surrendered, its army, consisting of millions of men, stretching out across much of Asia, was an ominous problem. No one could guarantee they would meekly hand over their guns. Some units might decide to fight on. Moreover, with the sudden collapse of the Japanese Empire, its governmental functions disintegrated, and a social implosion seemed possible throughout Asia. The Soviet Union might extend control over such a power vacuum. The United States had to move fast. Even hours spent mulling over difficult alternatives might have disastrous results.

When word reached Americans that Japan was surrendering, the War Department began to outline General

Order No. 1, a description of surrender procedures to be given the Japanese. The first paragraph, the Americans decided, should specify which Allied governments would accept the surrender of the various elements of the Japanese Imperial Army. Tired and frantic men in Washington, working under rigid deadlines, made geopolitical decisions involving a billion people. Their haphazard methods reveal an incredible example of faulty advance planning—or more precisely, of almost no prior planning at all.

The War Department had an Operations Division; this Operations Division had a Strategy and Planning Group; this Strategy and Planning Group had a Policy Section. And two members of the Policy Section produced the basic draft of that all-important opening paragraph. These two men were Colonel Charles H. Bonesteel and his assistant, Major Dean Rusk.

In a room by themselves sometime around midnight with a simple and rather small map of all of Asia, Bonesteel and Rusk began to consider surrender zones. The generals and admirals, in a room not far away, were impatient. The two men had orders to outline a plan in less than half an hour. They looked at the map. Rather than make subtle distinctions about national types and provincial lines, they decided to use simple methods. As far as Korea was concerned, they arrived at an easy solution. The map had latitudinal lines across it. It took but a moment to notice that if one used the Thirty-eighth Parallel as the dividing line for Korea's surrender zones, the Russians would be pent up near the Siberian border. The Thirty-ninth Parallel would be even farther north and therefore better, but one must be practical. Soviet troops were already in Manchuria and possibly Korea as well. American soldiers were hundreds of miles away and they could not arrive before the Russians. In fact the most practical arrangement might be to allow the Russians to accept the surrender of Japanese troops throughout all of Korea, but that alternative would be unacceptable to

39

Truman or most of his advisers. Given the fact that some
geographic compromise was inevitable, the Thirty-eighth
Parallel offered one particular advantage: Korea's two major
ports lay south of it and could be used by American forces
when they eventually arrived.

Soon after midnight on August 11 Bonesteel and Rusk
sent their plan to their superiors. It was accepted and
rushed upward through the committee hierarchy, until several days later it reached the desk of the president. Truman
approved it. [1]

Five years later, Private Kim Sun Ch'an, seventeen years
old, was a soldier in the army of the Democratic People's
Republic of Korea—a country Americans called North
Korea. Private Kim, a peasant, was neither very bright nor
very imaginative, although he had received six years of
rudimentary education. In the autumn of 1950 he was captured by American soldiers. Since he knew little military
information, his interrogation report consisted of a few
scant sentences, and after a military clerk typed these lines
Kim disappeared from the written weave of war and politics
which normally passes under the name of History.

Details about Kim's childhood are understandably vague,
but if one assumes he lived a "typical" Korean life, it probably went something like this: His family most likely farmed a
small plot of land, perhaps two to seven acres. Perhaps they
now owned it, but before 1945 it had probably been the
property of an absentee Japanese landlord. Since Kim was
born in northern Korea, he likely harvested beans, millet,
corn, or wheat; southern peasants generally grew rice. His
home probably had no furniture. Houses were meant to
provide warmth and protection from the elements, not com-
fort. The walls were no doubt made of mud, reinforced with
interlaced corn stalks; and beneath floors of packed dirt was
likely an *onder,* a system of flues running out from the
kitchen fireplace, heating the entire house. The usual Ko-

rean home had a tiny kitchen, dominated by that fireplace, and either one or two other rooms in which one sat, made love, played chess, and slept.

For meals Private Kim (no relation to any of the other Kims all over Korea, which has only a few family names) probably ate a monotonous cuisine, consisting mainly of rice boiled to a sticky pastelike consistency and a vegetable soup. In addition he might have drunk *suhnnuhn,* essentially a gently flavored rice broth. The people of Korea seldom had meat. When they did, they tended to slice it into tiny chunks, boil it until almost all the original flavor disappeared, then cover it with red pepper. (A ubiquitous taste delight was *kimchi,* a highly spiced pickled cabbage. Most westerners found it something less than a delicacy. Koreans loved it; they kept a special dark brown kimchi pot placed just outside the front door in a hole dug into the ground. Here in the cool earth the cabbage would become rich in its pickling juices.)

Such was probably the stuff of Kim's life: the eternal verities of the Asian peasant.

Early in 1950 North Korean authorities informed Kim that he was volunteering for the *Inmun Gun* (the "People's Army"). They told him that if he failed to enlist, his family would not receive their rice portion and he himself would be thrown into prison. Without hesitation Kim went to Pyongyang, the capital of his country, where on April 3, 1950, he was inducted. The government gave him a cheap green uniform which fitted him badly and Korean-made rubber sneakers. For a month and a half they trained him to lay telephone wire and install field phones for a howitzer company.

Kim was unhappy. He was the youngest in his company and the other eighty-five men made him run errands for them. (Koreans have little or no respect for youth.) To add to his misery, he was in Pyongyang only a few weeks when he received word his mother had just died. He was convinced she had literally worried herself to death over him. He was a lonely boy, far from home, ordered about by strangers.

On May 22, 1950, Private Kim, whose total service in the army had been seven weeks, boarded a train in Pyongyang, along with the rest of his unit, and rode south through the night. When the train stopped, horses dragged their four howitzers to a village called Chokkok-ni not far from the Thirty-eighth Parallel. In this hamlet Kim received a last few weeks' training.

The night of June 24 was very dark in Chokkok-ni. The *nyubai* (wet season) had begun, and clouds lay heavy and dank over the land. Before dawn a light mist fell along the 200-mile border between North and South Korea. It rained sporadically. Korean peasants on both sides of the border, unaware of the growing rumble of military vehicles, may have smiled to themselves in the night. Rain was good for the crops. It was a rice rain.

Sometime during the night the howitzer company—a tiny part of North Korea's crack Fourth Division—received its orders, and Kim Sun Ch'an, a seventeen-year-old boy with thick peasant feet and calloused hands, stood up and marched south. He carried a ball of soggy rice wrapped in a blue cloth, a tin cup, and a spoon. His government, the Democratic People's Republic, called him a patriotic defender of the mother soil. Within a few days American leaders would proclaim him a bloodthirsty Red puppet, part of a yellow horde of vicious Communist robots. He was wet and a little cold—and probably very frightened.[2]

The North Korean government Private Kim fought for, or at least lay down telephone lines for, arose from a political maelstrom stretching back into the earliest days of Japanese domination.[3]

Soon after Japan annexed Korea, a semiorganized underground developed, made up largely of young members of the bourgeoisie or the gentry. The Japanese made every effort to root it out. Members of the Japanese *kampetai,* the approximate oriental equivalent of the Gestapo, with the collaborationist support of carefully trained Korean policemen and a constant swarm of informers, made underground activities dangerously difficult. Countless Koreans faced horrid deaths in police basements. The names they murmured through broken lips before they died foretold executions for their fellows.

When a secret underground cell was cracked, therefore, its members usually fled to save their lives. Ultimately Korean émigrés spread all over Asia, perhaps 200,000 of them. Most went north across the Yalu River into Manchuria, then fanned out from there: some to Yenan in China to work with the anti-Japanese forces of Mao Tse-tung; some to Siberia to fight as part of the Russian army; some to Shanghai or Chungking, where conservative expatriates organized a Korean Provisional Government to lobby for support of the League of Nations. A few ended up as far away as Europe or the United States.

As a group, they did not represent a single, coherent force. Their backgrounds were diverse, their ambitions divided, their philosophies and goals represented the total spectrum of political and social ideologies. They were split into factions and clans and even families. They had no common bond beyond their hatred for the Japanese and their hunger for an independent Korea. None retained an overwhelming political base in the homeland.

When Russian and American armies entered Korea, these clangorous factions tumbled along in their wake. Meanwhile, several leaders who somehow had remained alive within Korea during the occupation bubbled to the surface. All of them—the returning émigrés, those who had remained at home—thought only in terms of the total motherland. None foresaw a division of their country; nor would they have condoned it. The geopolitical split at the

Thirty-eighth Parallel was not a function of *Korean* politics; it resulted from enmities between American and Soviet leaders. If the United States and the Soviet Union had stayed away from Korea, it is almost unimaginable that a division would have occurred. The factions certainly would have fought each other, but the whole of Korea would have been their prize. The cold war took the matter out of their hands.

The Russians, first on the scene, probably had no clear plan to erect a separate government in northern Korea, but they naturally hoped to implement some kind of *system* valuable to themselves. They utilized those Koreans sympathetic to Russian goals who could sustain some support from Koreans in general. The Russians were attempting a difficult balancing act—to find and support Korean leaders who had a power base of their own but were still malleable. They automatically excluded, of course, all conservative leaders. Koreans from the "Yenan faction," who had fought with Mao's army, remained suspect as perhaps too loyal to *Chinese* Communist goals and not perfectly in tune with those of the Soviet Union. Koreans who had spent any extended time in Russia were far too few to be significant. The Russians therefore were really left with only two groups: 1) leftists who had stayed in Korea during the occupation; 2) leaders of the "Kapsan faction," who had fought as guerrillas against the Japanese, usually in Manchuria. The Russians used representatives of both of them. But the mix was not perfect. Factionalism and jostling for political power became a constant part of North Korean politics from 1945 to 1950.[4]

The most powerful leader to emerge from the fire of North Korean politics was a heavy-set, round-faced man named Kim Il Sung. Born in 1912 in central Korea, the son of a middle-class schoolteacher, he was brought by his fleeing family to Manchuria to escape Japanese oppression around 1925.

Beyond such scraps of information little is known about this man. His enemies claim he was a minor Communist functionary who proved so unctuously subservient to Soviet dictates that he attracted the attention of Russian commissars looking for a Korean puppet. According to these sources, Kim Il Sung and the Russians fabricated heroic and marvelous stories to make him appear a national hero, when in fact he did little or nothing of note.

His supporters claim he joined the Communist party while still a teen-ager. They say that in 1931, when Japan grabbed Manchuria, he formed a small band of young guerrillas and fought the Japanese in a crusade lasting a decade. His idolatrous biography states that he and his followers fought over 100,000 battles (more than 20 a day) and they gloriously won every time.[5]

The probable truth is that he was a successful guerrilla leader in the Yalu River borderland between Manchuria and Korea. In 1941 he fled the region, just ahead of the Japanese police. He probably missed opportunities to escape south toward Mao's army and retreated north to Siberia. He apparently joined the Red Army, and perhaps, though this is debatable, fought alongside the Russians at Stalingrad.

Whatever his background and early life before 1945, certain things about him have become clear. He was an absolutely dedicated Communist, a Korean nationalist, and totally ruthless. His doughy face, despite its youthful appearance, was cruel and humorless. Its fleshy contours, like the soft moss covering the rocky hills of Korea, hid its hardness. It lacked the dignity of a Mao or a Ho Chi Minh, but it was a tenacious face. He was a relentless man who would outlive his opponents; he was a survivor.

Syngman Rhee was the president of the Republic of Korea, south of the Thirty-eighth Parallel. In his own way he was as tough and calculating as Kim Il Sung.

Rhee was born in 1875, a member of a family of local

gentry, during the last years of a decaying Korean dynasty that was riddled with inefficiency, anachronistic, and reactionary. He studied at a Methodist mission school, where he proved such a prize pupil it hired him to teach English. Western ideas reinforced his distaste for his own government. He became a reformer, and in the context of his time and place, a revolutionary. He was arrested and tortured. Police beat him with rods and whips. They placed bamboo between his fingers and tied them tightly together, so tightly the flesh sheared off from the tips. (In later years when he was tired or the weather brought back old pains he absently rubbed his fingers together.) He remained in prison for seven years before the government relented and freed him. [6]

After his release in 1904 he went to the United States. The Russians and the Japanese were fighting over which would take Korea. Rhee naively hoped to persuade President Theodore Roosevelt, who openly admired the Japanese, to support Korean independence. He soon realized the futility of his effort, but rather than sail home he began work in the United States on a series of college degrees culminating in a doctorate in political science from Princeton. He returned to Korea, but the Japanese had annexed his homeland and he left once more. For the next thirty years he lobbied for Korean autonomy—in the United States and in Geneva with the League of Nations.

He was a handsome man with a wide strong mouth, a straight aristocratic nose, and intelligent eyes carefully hooded behind their oriental folds. He knew the jargon of American liberalism, he understood the politics of Korea. But outside of missionary circles, most American leaders found his strident demands embarrassing. He seemed too intense.

Late in 1945 he returned to Korea. He was not some weak marionette coming home hidden in the baggage of the American army. He was a hardened old nationalist. He might wear western clothes, speak cultivated English, go to

Methodist services on Sunday, introduce foreigners to his Austrian wife, but he was completely Korean. At first he was only one of several prominent conservative or moderate émigrés reentering their own country after years of frustrating exile. Within a few years he stood alone. His rivals had either left for Pyongyang, accepted his supremacy, or died. His two chief competitors were assassinated. Both had seemed more moderate than he. There is no direct evidence that he ordered their killings, but their deaths were convenient to both him and his reactionary supporters, cadres of well-to-do and middle-class families who considered it their natural right to incorporate most of the good land abandoned by Japanese landlords.

Between 1945 and 1948 the United States governed South Korea. Times were difficult for Korea (as they were for most of Europe and Asia). The chief American administrator was Lieutenant General John R. Hodge, a man of good will but limited vision—with less intelligence and sensitivity than the position required. Hodge wanted to do "right," but from the Victorian confines of his gunboat diplomacy, "right" meant a conservative regime controlled by the United States. This was unacceptable to almost all Koreans, including Syngman Rhee.[7] Hodge seemed out of place, as if he had stepped through a time warp from nineteenth-century British India into the complicated politics of the mid–twentieth century. He stumbled from one faux pas to another. He once referred to Koreans as "the same breed of cats" as Japanese. (Rhee's fingertips must have tingled mightily.) His policies were confused and inconsistent—and often unpopular. He sold land in such a way that it ended up in the hands of the well-to-do. He used Korean policemen trained by the Japanese *kampetai*. His government was disastrously inane, a caricature of the worst kind of Western colonialism.[8]

Hodge was hardly all to blame. Inchoate planning by the American government had put the poor general in an impossible position, and the vacillations of America's Asian policies, partly understandable in light of its collapsing policy in China, merely made matters worse. The United States offered Koreans certain "political" reforms—like the concepts embodied in the Bill of Rights—but did not try to understand the complex economic and social problems facing that country. (In North Korea the Soviet Union condoned almost no political freedoms—which in a nation like Korea only seem to benefit the middle and upper classes— but provided extensive land distribution and relatively stable crop prices. The Russians, who kept a low profile, were never "popular" in the North, but they were not nearly as detested as Americans were in the South.)

In 1947 the United States, with a sigh of relief, turned over the problem to the United Nations, and in the summer of 1948 the Republic of Korea was born. Dr. Syngman Rhee became its first president. America withdrew its military forces the following year (more than six months after Russian troops left the Democratic People's Republic). Under an agreement with Rhee's government the Americans left a small group of military "advisers." (In later years this term would come to mean many things, some of them sinister and malevolent, but at the time these advisers were strictly that: Their duties were to help the South Koreans create a modern organized army.)

Rhee and his supporters produced a government which was hardly a model republic. Its members took no serious action against, and possibly even encouraged, a rampant inflation. The black market operated openly. The government, moreover, was oppressive. Its minister of education purged the Korean school system of thousands of politically suspect teachers. Another minister, Chang Taik Sang, previously chief of police in Seoul, had possibly once been the country's chief torturer. In fact his brutality apparently became so infamous that he was investigated by Rhee's government, then *promoted* to minister of foreign affairs. The

government's minister of home affairs declared, "The torturing of Communists is not to be criticized." The Republic
of Korea suppressed opposition newspapers and arrested
political opponents. In September 1949 the Home Ministry
reported that more than 36,000 political prisoners were in
jail. Prisoners who escaped and were recaptured were shot
and left on the doorsteps of recalcitrant opponents, apparently as object lessons. [9]

Several facts should be noted on Rhee's behalf. Democracy is an immensely slippery concept, even in the best of
circumstances. In the midst of rapid social and economic
changes it is even more elusive. "Opposition" in a country
like Korea is not necessarily "loyal." Loyalty, too, can be a
complicated emotion, made up of strands that bind one to
soil and family and friends, to individual leaders, to religion,
to ideas, even to government. Given Korea's recent un-
natural division, with thousands of families separated only
by an imaginary boundary, a "shakedown" of some sort
could be expected. Korean loyalties had been snarled by the
creation of two new governments, each claiming to be the
only representative voice of the people, yet each tainted by
its attachment to foreign ideas and outside powers. In a
situation like this how does a government determine which
of its citizens are faithful—for that matter, which of its
soldiers, which of its governmental leaders? Everyone must
be watched. Wariness and suspicion become a normal function of government. Brutality appears necessary to the existence of the state. (Such a condition would have been as true
above the Thirty-eighth Parallel as below. South Korea's
purges were noted outside the country and condemned,
North Korea's went unreported. It would be naive to assume, especially of a nation with a long history of violence
and savagery, that the Democratic People's Republic did not
practice torture on a relatively broad scale.)

Rhee's government in reality did face a violent internal
threat. Anti-Rhee underground agents burrowed deeply into

South Korea. The North Korean government trained special guerrillas at a place called Kang-Dong Political Institute on the outskirts of Pyongyang. Graduates of this school, perhaps a hundred a month, slipped south across the border and disappeared into the population.[10] A mysterious middle-aged man calling himself Chief Namdo was apparently one of them. He began organizing peasant guerrillas in the mountainous region along the east coast in 1948. By the time war broke out and fogged the records, he had a band of followers 200 strong.[11]

Twice between 1948 and 1949 guerrillas in South Korea mounted major offenses. Beginning in March 1949 Rhee's soldiers began a systematic search-and-destroy sweep of the countryside, burning the huts and fields of any mountain people even suspected of harboring guerrillas.[12] (One must wonder how much of these actions by both the mountain people and the army were the result of ancient enmities between highlanders and lowlanders, hatreds that seem to crop up in almost every such society.) These efforts, while tremendously bloody, were apparently successful. One of the most surprising facets of the early days of the war in 1950 was that no guerrilla uprising, nor any significant sabotage, coincided with the northern attack.[13]

Rhee did allow a certain amount of parliamentary freedom, even when it drifted against him. On May 30, 1950 (less than four weeks before the war), South Koreans went to the polls to elect new members of the National Assembly, in probably the most democratic election in their history, both before or since. The result was a major defeat for Rhee and his right-wing supporters, who collected only 67 of the 210 seats. It is impossible to know what might have occurred if war had not come and made him a symbolic rallying point, allowing him to solidify his position once more.

Within hours of the beginning of the Korean War, the government of North Korea claimed that its army only crossed the border to parry a surprise attack from South Korea. Over the years North Korea's claim has found occasional proponents. Syngman Rhee, they say, in the months before June 1950, made secret deals with a loose international coalition of conservatives, including Chiang Kai-shek, John Foster Dulles, and Douglas MacArthur.[14]

Chiang's regime in China had collapsed less than a year earlier. He retreated to Formosa, but Mao's army was massing for an amphibious invasion which would inevitably sweep him aside. Only one thing could save him: the direct intervention of the United States. Without it, Chiang Kai-shek was doomed. Truman's government, however, had clearly written Chiang off and was merely waiting for his final curtain calls before shifting into a position to deal with Mao. According to advocates of the conspiracy theory, Chiang perceived that a war in Korea would force Truman to alter his position.

John Foster Dulles in 1950 served as an emissary for the State Department, sent to Asia to outline a treaty with Japan. While there, he flew to Seoul to give a stirring speech promising American support to the National Assembly. Dulles was a spokesman for a brand of conservative Republicanism formed by a combination of tough anti-communism and Protestant missionary instincts. He took his religion seriously, which partly explains his admiration for both Chiang and Rhee. "No matter what you say about the President of Korea and the President of Nationalist China," he once said, "those two gentlemen are modern-day equivalents of the founders of the church. They are Christian gentlemen who have suffered for their faith. They have been steadfast and upheld the faith in a manner which entitles them to be considered in the category of the early leaders of the church."[15] The conspiracy advocates suggest that Dulles might have helped plan a war which eventually did in fact preserve the regimes of both those "Christian gentlemen."

MacArthur hated communism and sympathized with Chiang. He despised Truman's Asian policies as vacillating and dangerous, and he wanted a tougher stand against communism in Asia.

Proponents of the conspiracy theory, furthermore, suggest it was no accident that Secretary of Defense Louis A. Johnson and Chairman of the Joint Chiefs of Staff Omar N. Bradley (who had just been in Formosa talking to Chiang) were in Tokyo when John Foster Dulles (who had just returned from Seoul) was there.

Rhee himself was openly in favor of an attack upon the North. As a nationalist he wanted to unify all his people; as a shrewd politician he must have recognized that a successful war would rally support for his weakened government. But even though his army, now well over 100,000 men, was increasing at a great rate, he did not have the weapons, especially both tanks and planes, to begin a solid offensive. (It was no secret that Washington withheld these arms for that very reason.[16])

The conspiracy theorists suggest that early in the morning of June 25 Rhee secretly sent an armed probe against a town named Haeju, just across the Parallel. This, they suggest, jolted the North Koreans into a counterattack, made by Rhee to seem a shocking invasion of his peaceful country, and used by MacArthur and his ilk to stir Washington into action.

The most serious flaw in this scenario, in addition to the fact that it is based more on conjecture than hard evidence, is that the North Korean army advanced in seven major coordinated prongs along a 200-mile front, including an amphibious invasion of the east coast by motorized junks. Furthermore, during the weeks before June 25, the North Korean army transported civilians living just above the Parallel several miles northward. (In South Korea they knew about this withdrawal of civilians, of course, but they concluded it was merely a method, already used elsewhere by the Russians, of creating a no-man's-land, making it easier to detect crossing spies and refugees. [17])

Such facts seem to prove that the Democratic People's Republic attacked first. Yet curious inconsistencies remain. The most startling of these is that only about *half* the North Korean army took part in the initial attack. Why? There are several persuasive possibilities. [18]

A civil war was inevitable in Korea. Each side hated the other. Both were expanding their armies rapidly and spoke repeatedly of unifying the whole Korean nation by arms. Clashes along the border were frequent and bloody, and sometimes involved as many as several thousand men on either side. Rumors spread that war was coming. Perhaps North Korea, with its smaller population, became afraid that if nothing were done to forestall it, the South's military forces would eventually become so much larger that when war did break out, Rhee's side would win. A sudden blow now, while the ROK (Republic of Korea) army still remained relatively weak, might topple Rhee's regime. The North Koreans, whose political theories were remarkably immature, may have assumed that Rhee's recent election defeat indicated South Koreans rejected the Republic itself and would welcome the People's Army. A general assault with a strong jab against Seoul might therefore succeed. If the Republic were wobbly, six divisions should be enough.

The timing of the attack is more questionable. There seems little doubt that North Korea had planned an offensive for August, and most likely initiated it earlier because of a power struggle within North Korea.

Kim Il Sung's chief rival in North Korea was a man named Pak Hon-yong, who had led the Communist movement inside Korea during the dangerous days of the occupation. Pak was a national hero with powerful support within the Party. Kim and Pak vied bitterly within the Party for prestige. One or the other of these two rivals probably instigated the attack to gain status within the ruling committees of the government, that is, one of them may have pulled the trigger early to outmaneuver the other. Each had enough influence to push the assault; which one did may never be known. After the war Pak was tried by a North Korean tribunal and executed. Was this because he—responsible before the war for overseeing the guerrillas—had overestimated their supportive effect? Or because he had overstated the weakness of Rhee's regime? Or because he himself had initiated the attack and had somehow bypassed Kim? There is no answer yet.

The controversy over who fired first and why, like many such historical riddles, may never be settled. The truth lies caught somewhere within the web of lies and contradictions that make up history. No matter. The question of who began the Korean civil war soon proved less important than who was going to win it.

CHAPTER FOUR

Something
Surprising

Possibly this influence will hold off until tomorrow but few people will
pass through the next three days without something surprising and of a
pleasant nature coming their way.

—Horoscope column, *Hartford Courant*
(June 25, 1950)

JOHN J. MUCCIO LIKED Spanish love songs, to sing the sad,
longing words of devotion in liquid Castilian, a language he
had learned at the American embassy in Panama. He was
now ambassador to the Republic of Korea, a position requir-
ing immense tact and delicacy. Muccio was right for the job:
He was absolutely genial and pleasant, a perfect man to
invite to a party. He had a nice rumpled face, etched with
laugh lines and a dimple in his chin. He always brushed his
wavy, slightly graying hair toward the back of his head and
generally sported factory-tied bow ties. He was a dapper
dresser (like Truman) without being too dapper or foppish.
He looked a little like an aging Rudy Vallee with glasses. He
held his liquor well; he told good jokes and witty stories; he
was a bachelor and liked pretty ladies, but was never openly
licentious or slavering. He was good company.

Born in Italy and brought up in Rhode Island near Provi-
dence, he went to Brown University. He drifted awhile,
then entered the diplomatic corps; by 1950 he had served for

more than twenty years. He was neither the smoothest nor the most brilliant nor the richest ambassador in America's service. Nor was he the most energetic (he almost totally refused to do paperwork). But he was sincerely devoted to his job and took care to do it to the best of his somewhat limited abilities.

His affability was a valuable attribute for foreign service. At times he reminds one of that classic diplomat Talleyrand, of whom Napoleon once said you could kick him in the buttocks and the smile on his face would never change. Muccio had an almost oriental ability to ignore problems until most of them faded away, an excellent trait in a place like Seoul. Most important, he liked Koreans. He got along well with them and they apparently liked him. [1]

He was head of a large and awkward bureaucracy called the American Mission in Korea (AMIK), consisting of about 1,300 men and women, the largest State Department mission in the world, in fact the largest American administrative unit overseas anywhere. [2] Americans connected to AMIK ran the whole occupational spectrum. There were barbers and butchers, dieticians and engineers, economists, teachers, and radio announcers. There were secretaries and chauffeurs and electricians and librarians. There were espionage agents and counterespionage agents. And there were the 500 military advisers. Some were dedicated, honest, and capable—but unfortunately many were mediocre and worse.

Korea was a backwash of the American bureaucracy. Members of the Economic Cooperation Administration (ECA) or the United States Information Service (USIS)— and their families—would have much preferred prestige duty in Europe, or even Japan. Here in Korea the plumbing was primitive, the cuisine unappetizing, the electric system haphazard at best, and the Koreans themselves, my dear, made such wretched servants. Maddening, inefficient little buggers, you know, and dishonest too.

Most Americans in Seoul disliked Korea. They isolated

themselves in their compounds and PXs. The United States government owned 375 houses in Seoul and supplied them, furnished and rent-free, to high-ranking American families, along with three (later two) servants. (At one point 8,000 Koreans officially worked for AMIK. By June 1950 they had been reduced to 5,000. This number does not include those hired independently by American families.) The highest salary for Koreans was $16.00 per month, which was less than some Korean industries paid. Lower-ranking Americans lived in the five embassy-owned hotels. The American government also provided a beauty parlor, a barber shop, a liquor store, and free taxi service (predecessor of the modern government limousine). Despite all these perquisites, since so many Americans considered themselves sentenced to a hardship post, they often became irascible, petty, and vicious. One American wife, discovering her house had previously been occupied by an American of Korean descent, demanded a change to a "cleaner" building—and received it. Squabbling within the Mission, and between Americans and Koreans, was constant.

Heavy drinking within the American community was common. Since most Americans refused to leave their residences in Seoul to visit the countryside or talk to the people, there often seemed to be nothing else to do but gather in the lounges of one of the embassy hotels. (A government inspector, sent from Washington, once became so drunk himself he passed out in Muccio's parlor.) But the chief problem with AMIK was that it was filled with incompetents; it was eaten out from within like a house with termites. As one correspondent once said about the military advisers, "Korea was the 'Siberia' of the Far East Command, a dumping ground for every misfit, gold brick, and incompetent west of Hawaii."[3] Some of the Mission were bunglers; a few were unsavory, making money on the side by various hustles: black marketeering, construction graft, smuggling, and under-the-table sales of government equipment.

Military-based government lends itself to a certain amount of corruption, and even though AMIK was superficially civilian it depended on the army for much of its support—including the fact that all Americans used military scrip in downtown Seoul. Though the naked presence of the American army permeated everything, few American soldiers were actually stationed in Korea, and these generally wished they were somewhere else. Almost none had volunteered for this duty; they were "levied" from other units elsewhere. Since good soldiers are normally shielded by their commanding officers as too precious to be let go, inevitably those who filtered into Korea were often of poor caliber. One colonel conceded, "Korea was considered a very undesirable assignment. Those [officers] on duty in Korea wanted to get out."[4] Even the official history of this Korean Military Advisory Group—and military accounts are notorious for their bureaucratic neutrality—states that many of the officers were too young and inexperienced for this sort of work. "Although excellent and promising otherwise," it says, "all were not qualified to advise Korean regimental and division commanders, who by culture and training were prone to regard youth as callow and beneath notice."[5]

A few other Americans, unconnected to AMIK, did live and work in Korea. Businessmen, especially those associated with import-export firms, began to arrive. Though the Korean economy was erratic, or perhaps because it was, a canny investor could make some money.

Missionaries formed a much more visible group. About the year 1600, following a period of ravaging wars, Korea hunkered down into a somnolent state of isolation and refused to deal with foreigners. Outsiders called her the Hermit Kingdom. Then, starting in 1882, she slowly opened herself up to trade and new ideas. American missionaries were among the first foreigners to enter. They served as that nation's first modern doctors and educators, its experts on hygiene, sewers, and water usage. (Some Americans have become suspicious of the missionary ethos, linking it—often correctly—with rigid Victorian morality, greed, and racism. Undoubtedly some missionaries in Korea have fitted that description, but many have lived in relative poverty, giving of themselves. Few have been as supercilious and remote from the Korean nation as were most members of AMIK. Missionaries learned the subtleties of the Korean language and came to understand and love the people. Of course they tried to convert the Koreans to Christianity, and possibly we should blame them for that, for attempting to alter the ancient Korean value system to coincide with Western religion. Yet, in balance, the human good they did greatly outweighs their potential cultural harm.)

As missionaries they were certainly successful. In 1950 there were 290 Protestant churches in Seoul alone; many of them were connected to hospitals, schools, and universities. It is estimated that Korea had 660,000 Christians in 1948.[6]

A more immediate example of the impact of the missions turned up one day two weeks after the Korean War began. Charred signs of devastation and war spread everywhere; refugees filled the roads. In a tiny village an American found a can of vegetable soup. A label on the can said, "Jeannette Kazaal, first grade, Immaculate Heart Academy, Tucson, Ariz."[7]

Saturday, June 24, 1950, was sunny and bright in Seoul. The sky was a clear, glistening blue; the air was warm, softened by quiet breezes. A day for weddings and picnics, for patio parties where the clink of frosty ice in good Scotch plays background accompaniment to merry laughter. A day of friendship and love. Of peace.

Later on, members of the American community remembered the lingering harmony of that day. Their lives, for a moment calm and happy, are captured in poignancy as in the yellowed photograph of the wedding party in its now outdated finery, its faces wreathed in shy and awkward smiles, staring stiffly at the camera. (We look sadly at that picture from the past, knowing what came afterward. This one there is dead, that one insane. Over there, the man with the huge grin is now an incurable alcoholic. And the marriage, of course, went sour. He beat her, she slept around, they are divorced. And so it goes.)

But for a last few hours on that Saturday Americans relaxed. It had rained sporadically for several days, then stopped for this one last moment before the rainy season began in earnest. Threats of attack from the North had become so frequent of late, with nothing really happening, that war jitters had subsided in AMIK. (In 1949, for instance, there had been 660 border incidents.) Alerts and curfews were a normal part of Seoul life. Just three weeks earlier AMIK had expected a major assault. And nothing had occurred. One's psyche can tense up for a state of readiness just so often; one becomes blasé about threats which are never carried out. [8]

At Kimpo Airport, not far from downtown Seoul, a Northwest Airlines plane taxied in late in the morning. A small crowd of Americans were gathered, most of them to say goodbye to a popular young couple, Ralph and Sally Fisher, returning to the States after their duty in Korea. As the Fishers prepared to get on the plane amid the laughter and fluttering hands of farewell, few probably noticed a group of teachers from Illinois Tech who must have nervously stepped off the plane and shouldered their way through the crowd. They were here at the invitation of the Economic Cooperation Administration, a wing of AMIK, to teach trade skills at a new technological training center. They were probably filled with curiosity and excitement about their new posts in exotic Korea. [9]

Near the Han River, which circles just beneath the city, the Sobingo Gun Club, a skeet- and trap-shooting group, had a contest. In the afternoon some Americans went south by rail to a tiny beach resort a few of them were building into a vacation spa. At the Seoul Union Club two young missionaries got married. Across town American children shouted and splashed in the embassy pool.[10]

Late in the day, as the shadows lengthened across the patios and roof gardens, Americans prepared for their evening's entertainment. The band at the Officers' Club warmed up, readying itself for the usual Saturday night dance. The bars filled. Taxis chauffeured handsomely dressed couples here and there as the social swirl increased its tempo.

During the afternoon Kristian Jensen, an aging Methodist missionary, had attended the wedding at the Seoul Union Club. Now he headed out of town to visit the mission at Kaesong, a village only a few hundred yards from the Parallel. Within a few hours he—and five Kaesong missionaries—would be swallowed up by war. Not all would survive. One would die in North Korean captivity; the other five, including Jensen, would return after the war, worn and tired.[11]

Sometime that evening Jack James, veteran reporter, checked in at the embassy pressroom to see if anything was stirring. He had a friend in G-2 (Intelligence) and there was scuttlebutt of a possible invasion at almost any moment. He concluded, however, it was a false alarm. He decided he would come back the next day and file a report that, despite rumors of war, all was quiet along the South Korean border.[12]

By four o'clock Sunday morning most of the revelers and travelers and missionaries and reporters were in bed.

It started to rain.

War began on the far western corner of the Parallel. Then, during a period lasting several hours, like a series of firecrackers laid out along a single fuse, it crackled sporadically eastward until it inflamed the entire border. North Korea attacked with about 90,000 men, including a whole range of military technology: 7 infantry divisions, a motorcycle regiment, 150 tanks, and a brigade of border constabulary. They even launched an amphibious attack on the east coast.

The assault opened with an artillery barrage. For half an hour howitzers and mortars coughed. Finally a moment of silence. Then the onslaught—men on foot, by truck, by tank, by motorcycle, by ship, and in one section where they repaired a broken track, by railway car. [13]

In several sectors they broke through. They had the advantage of surprise and the weight of numbers. About a third of the ROK army was on leave that Sunday morning, and most of the American advisers were spending the weekend in Seoul. [14] In one sector a single South Korean regiment, probably outnumbered at least five to one, faced the two best divisions of the Inmun Gun. Little wonder the line sagged.

Later on, Americans had the impression that there had been an immediate rout, that the ROK army had scattered, that the North Koreans had almost meandered south like vacationers on a picnic. In reality the first three days of the war were tangled. Battle lines became what military men call "fluid." On the two far flanks, touching the sea on either side, ROK troops—badly outnumbered—gradually and successfully withdrew according to plans they had made months before. But both sectors were incidental: The key to the fighting lay in control of the three main highways running north-and-south through the middle of the peninsula. North Korea had placed her best-trained soldiers here in the center—and thrust them straight ahead.

As the fighting began, the few Americans attached to each ROK unit called their headquarters with the information. Around six o'clock a KMAG (Korean Military Advisory Group) radio operator in Seoul received a message from American advisers near the far western corner of the Parallel. The operator wrote down the report and passed it on.

Most likely he was unexcited, since similar messages had come in so often.[15]

By about seven, however, KMAG began to change its mind. ROK headquarters was right next door in the same building and reports were pouring in there from all along the line. KMAG officers, getting snatches from their own men in the field and from the ROK messages, became concerned. They were not sure yet what it meant, but the situation seemed critical enough to spread the news along. They called the military attaché at the embassy; he in turn phoned Everett Drumright, the chief deputy there. Drumright, tall, hardworking, humorless, the classic civil servant, decided not to wake Ambassador Muccio until he had more information. He told the attaché, Bob Edwards, to keep him informed.

Edwards drove to the embassy office, situated for lack of anything better on one of the top floors of the Banto, Seoul's largest hotel. He and his assistant carefully sifted the growing deluge of reports. Others attached to the embassy began to arrive.

Sometime around eight o'clock the reporter Jack James drove his United Press jeep to the Banto. He later claimed he had expected to go to a picnic that afternoon and only stopped at the chancery to pick up his raincoat, which he had overlooked the night before. He recalls: "As I ran through the rain toward the door of the embassy, an intelligence officer who is a friend of mine came out hastily looking for his car and driver. He thought I was on the story. [The friend was probably Bob Edwards on his way to KMAG headquarters to be closer to the action.]

"'What do you hear from the border?' he asked me.

"'Not very much yet. What do you hear?' I said.

"'Hell, they're supposed to have crossed everywhere except in the Eighth Division area,' he told me.

"'That's more than I've heard,' I said and went into the press room to start phoning."

At first James was dubious and called some of his American and Korean sources. The moment must have been incredibly exhilarating to him. Here he was, all alone, in an empty pressroom, the only sounds his own hushed telephone conversations, an occasional isolated call back to him confirming his ripening suspicions that a real war had begun; the rush of excited footsteps back and forth in the chancery hallways; and the wash of rain outside against the windows. It was a journalist's dream: a total, unmitigated scoop on the world about the beginning of a war. Best of all, he had the time by himself to be absolutely sure. No other reporters disturbed his isolation. He asked his sources not to tell any other correspondents what was happening. They agreed. Another reporter, who must have heard that something was going on, called one of James's sources about nine o'clock but was told everything was quiet.

James kept checking with the military officers at the chancery; he even drove over to ROK headquarters for a moment, then rushed back to the pressroom to make more telephone calls. Finally, he sat at one of the pressroom desks, blackened by coffee rings and cigarette burns, and clacked out his story on a typewriter. He checked it over carefully, and waited for more collaboration.

Meanwhile, Bob Edwards called Drumright again. He said, while he could not be positive, that his information indicated a full-scale assault. Drumright decided he could wait no longer and phoned Muccio at his home, a lovely oriental house with lacquered beams and beautifully finished woodwork.

"Brace yourself for a shock," Drumright said. "The Communists are hitting all along the front."

"Let's go to the office," Muccio replied at once.

Within minutes the two arrived at the chancery. Jack James saw the ambassador and cagily asked him why he was there, hoping to get more confirmation.

"I'm checking on a report I've received that the Communists are striking all along the Parallel," Muccio replied, and went into his office.

Around nine-thirty someone at the chancery told James that the embassy was about to "let Washington know about this."

"If it's good enough for you to file," the reporter answered with relief, "it's good enough for me."

He donned his raincoat and drove several blocks to the cable office. He marked the bulletin "urgent." It was time-dated 9:50. After double-checking the cable's wording, like a reluctant mother about to see her child leave home, finally he let it go out, then ran back to his jeep and returned to the pressroom. More confirmation came in. At ten-thirty he sent a second bulletin reemphasizing the first, this time "without qualifications."

Ironically, within a few minutes his UP cable sped to New York, from there to Tangier, then on to Manila, and finally back to Seoul where it was translated into Korean. It appeared on the streets as a UP bulletin in Seoul's Sunday morning newspapers.

O. H. P. King, a friend of James's and a rival, was the A.P. representative in Seoul. King had been out carousing with James until late the night before, and on Sunday morning he slept in. He was wakened by a stinging message from his editor in the United States, asking, in effect, why the UP had gotten a jump of several hours on the Associated Press.

(Since he went to bed quite late the night before, why was Jack James up so early? Why did he need a raincoat for a picnic? Most likely what happened was this: His "friend in G-2," maybe Bob Edwards, probably called him as soon as the first reports came in. James probably lied about the raincoat to protect his friend. Intelligence officers can get in trouble for revealing that kind of information to a reporter.)

About the same time Jack James was telling the newspaper-reading world about Korea, Muccio was sending a message to the State Department marked "Night Action" (used only during emergencies). "According to Korean Army reports which are partly confirmed by Korean Military Advisory Group field adviser reports," Muccio carefully reported, "North Korean forces invaded Republic of Korea territory at several points this morning." He stated the little he knew and concluded, "It would appear from the nature of the attack and the manner in which it was launched that it constitutes an all-out offensive against the Republic of Korea."[16]

The use of the word "invaded" in Muccio's message is interesting. The attitude it reveals was common among Americans, who consistently viewed the two parts of Korea as totally separate entities. From the Korean point of view—in either North or South—the attack was not normally considered an "invasion." It is hardly an invasion to move from one place in one's nation to another, even when attacking with an army. Many Koreans living in the North were born below the Parallel, and the reverse was true. The connotations of the word "invasion" do not fit their attitudes. As far as Northerners were concerned, they were merely ridding their land of a repellent foreign-backed regime, newly created and without any claims to tradition or permanence. One "invades" someone else's property; it implies an intrusion. To view the North Korean assault as an invasion is to misconstrue its meaning, to view it from the wrong perspective. As American officials used the word, it indicated a conceptual mistake they continuously made about Korea—and over the next two decades about Vietnam.

Despite all the fluttering activity at the chancery, most Americans in Seoul spent that morning unaware of the war, lolling in bed or relaxing on this peaceful sabbath. One American, John Caldwell, an official with the Information Service (USIS), later remembered that he went into his garden about nine in the morning and chatted with his

Korean gardener. "We stood and talked, gloating over the rainfall and, like the earth, absorbing the longed-for damp." Above him, he heard the rumble of a plane flying low in the heavy cloud bank. That afternoon he and his wife and some guests brunched on cakes and coffee, and chatted about Caldwell's collection of pottery and porcelain. The telephone rang and disturbed their world with news of war. [17]

At one o'clock Muccio released a bulletin to WVTP, the embassy radio station. It stated:

> Stand by for a special announcement.
>
> WVTP has been authorized by the Ambassador to make the following announcement.
>
> At 4 o'clock this morning, North Korean armed forces began unprovoked attacks against defense positions of the Republic of Korea at several points along the 38th degree parallel. . . . Both Korean officials and the security forces are handling the situation calmly and with ability. There is no reason for alarm. . . . [18]

This message was repeated, without much change, throughout the day.

Arthur Bunce, head of ECA in Seoul, planned to give a cocktail party that afternoon. He wanted to introduce his colleagues to the teachers from Illinois Tech who had arrived at Kimpo the night before. Bunce had to cancel his party. The teachers left Korea two days later and went home.

Koreans in Seoul seemed buoyant and optimistic. Military movement throughout the city was energetic.

Jeeps with loudspeakers raced through the streets, announcing to all soldiers, "Join your units immediately." Military policemen commandeered all privately owned buses and trucks. Convoys of trucks shot through town heading north, with troops, nets over their helmets camouflaged with leaves and twigs, holding precariously to their sides. Throngs of citizens crowded street corners, cheering each military vehicle as it rushed by. [19]

Caldwell felt curiously drawn toward the center of the city. He recalls: "I spent several hours during the day down on the street in front of the Severance Hospital compound, watching the troops move forward, singing, and while they passed the crowds cheered. I could not help a lump in my throat: all differences seem to have been forgotten; white-clad farmer and businessman dressed Western style, both stood together behind their army."[20]

During the early morning South Korean officials seemed confident. They talked of taking the offensive—they hoped the attack might give them the opportunity. An official at the Defense Ministry said the first evening that the Inmun Gun was "still green and inexperienced." He boasted that "by tomorrow morning we shall have defeated them completely. Our only cause for dissatisfaction is that there has been no order to advance into the North."[21]

At first during the morning ROK troops had—in places—stopped the Inmun Gun. In sectors where South Korean units were near or at full strength, and *where they did not have to face tanks directly,* they not only held the North Koreans but even forced them to pull back. But in most places along the line they began to retreat.

The main reason probably lay in the fact that North Koreans had tanks, and South Korean soldiers were not prepared for them. They had no mines, their bazookas were ineffective, and they discovered to their horror that their artillery shells merely bounced off the thick steel walls. They tried everything. Some leaped on the tanks and attempted to pry open the hatches; others slithered up to the sides and shoved charges into them. A few volunteers even tied explosives to their bodies and dashed themselves beneath the treads. Perhaps ninety South Koreans died on one or the other of these antitank missions. Yet their suicidal tactics had little effect; they failed to stop more than a handful. Soon there were no more volunteers.

By the end of the first day the North Korean army had

punched holes in several places along the border. The situation for the Republic of Korea was not yet desperate but something had to be done fast.

A monstrously fat man named General Chae Pyong Dok made a crucial decision in the first hours of the war. Chae, about 5'6" and 245 pounds, called "Fat" Chae (or just "Fat Boy") by Americans, was chief of his country's army. Soon after word arrived at his headquarters about the assault, he drove to the front, watched for a while, and ordered two of his best divisions to counterattack the next morning against a critical point thirty miles above Seoul. It was an impossible, inane plan. One of the two divisions was already taking the brunt of the attack, and the other was in Taejon, over a hundred and twenty miles to the south. This second one would have to assemble, gather its equipment, transport itself (10,000 strong) by cantankerous trains to the front lines, and then strategically prepare itself for an attack. Parts of the Taejon division would arrive during the night, but by dawn only a fraction of it would be in place. The rest would be strung back a hundred miles. They would arrive bit by bit during the day, to be thrown into battle as isolated units, each badly outnumbered. Chae's order was a military nightmare. [22]

General Lee Hyung Koon commanded the Taejon division. Lee recognized the flaws in Chae's plans and tried without success to talk the rotund general out of them. When he failed at persuasion, he did something which only compounded the problem. He spent the day gathering his men and sending them north. He and his headquarters then headed for the Parallel and ensconced themselves near the front. He decided not to attack the next morning, but chose to wait in defensive positions to allow the rest of his division to gather around him. He did this without telling Chae of his decision—nor the other division, which attacked as ordered in the morning in the belief it had full support on its flank from Lee's division.

Late in the morning General Lee's troops, after watching artillery shells ricochet harmlessly off unscathed tanks, realizing they were increasingly outnumbered by North Korean soldiers moving at them, retreated into the hills on either side. The other ROK division, caught in a completely unprotected salient, had to withdraw. The combination of Chae's nonsensical plans and Lee's refractory sulkiness helped accomplish a military disaster. Shortly afterward, the entire South Korean army had to pull back. And once an army begins to retreat before an advancing foe, once it has started to leave its weapons and equipment behind, it becomes extremely hard to regroup.

The war was not lost yet. North Korean supply lines were stretching farther and farther. The ROK army had not by any means been destroyed, either in fact or in its morale. If it could just hold the Inmun Gun for a moment, maybe it could gather itself back together and press north again. It would need more supplies. It would need immediate aid against the tanks.

It would need help from the United States.

CHAPTER FIVE

Serious News

An atmosphere of tension, unparalleled since the war days, spread over the Capital.

—*New York Times*
(June 26, 1950)

SATURDAY NIGHT, U.S.A.

Americans played, totally unaware of the war in far-off Korea. At Palisades Amusement Park in New Jersey a happy, attractive lady won the local title of Mrs. America. Teen-agers, wandering toward the park's huge pool, watched bovinely for a moment and walked on. About six o'clock that evening, eight hundred miles away, Yogi Berra hit a home run in the ninth inning.

Television viewers laughed at the antics of Lucille Ball and Desi Arnez doing a guest spot on the Ken Murray show. At nine o'clock stay-at-homes examined their TV schedules, noted that the dark-eyed and clear-voiced singer Anna Maria Alberghetti was to be that evening's main attraction on "Cavalcade of Stars."

Outside, the moon was almost full and glowed quietly in the sky. Lovers, lying on the grass, stared upward. Some may have noticed that a little after nine, Mars became visible in the southwest.

When the New York headquarters of the United Press received Jack James's message, it immediately phoned its Washington office and told it to check out the story with government officials. The Washington office called the State Department but no one there knew anything. Finally, at 9:04 Donald Gonzales of UP phoned W. Bradley Connors at home. Connors was the public affairs officer for the State Department's Bureau of Far Eastern Affairs; his job was to deal with the press on just such matters. [1] Connors decided to contact his immediate superior, Dean Rusk, assistant secretary of state for Far Eastern affairs.

Rusk was in Georgetown at Joseph Alsop's that Saturday evening. Alsop, a journalist, was the favored scion of a wealthy old American family. He had used his money, his connections, and his urbane, occasionally acerbic wit to develop a web of friendships and contacts in government. His dinner parties attracted not only the brightest people in Washington, like young Congressman John F. Kennedy, but the highest-ranking as well. At the moment Dean Rusk—hardworking, considerate, gentlemanly, the soft and pleasant drawl of Georgia in his voice—was recognized by such cognoscenti as Alsop as an important personage at State. Rusk was a poor boy who had made it by brains and conscientious effort. He had spent much of his career specializing in either Asian affairs or United Nations matters. (This combination was about to be very important during the next few hours.) He had only had the job of assistant secretary of state for Far Eastern affairs for two months.

During the previous spring Senator Joe McCarthy had discovered the journalistic appeal of Red-baiting. He had focused his assault on the State Department in general and the Far Eastern desk in particular. For this reason, among others, Walton Butterworth, the head of that section, resigned. Rusk at the time was deputy undersecretary, officially higher in rank than Butterworth, but he agreed to take the Far Eastern spot. "I fit it," he told Secretary of

State Dean Acheson, who replied, "You get the Purple Heart and the Congressional Medal of Honor all at once for this."[2]

Just before Connors reached him at Alsop's house, Rusk and his host were discussing tensions between Yugoslavia and the Soviet Union. When Connors' call came in, Rusk excused himself and went to the phone. He quietly told the young public affairs officer to call Muccio in Seoul and find out what was happening there. He himself would go to State and await developments. After he put down the phone, he held a brief, whispered conversation with another of Alsop's guests, Secretary of the Army Frank Pace, Jr. Both of them apologized and left the party at the same time. (An observer as canny as Joe Alsop must have assumed something big was happening—probably in China—and most likely made some discreet phone calls as soon as they left.)

United Press reporters continued to call government officials for information or for their reactions to James's report from Korea. About ten, for instance, they phoned Omar Bradley, chairman of the Joint Chiefs of Staff, who had just returned from a tour of Asia a few hours before.[3] They also called Louis Johnson, secretary of defense, who had been with Bradley on the tour.[4] Neither knew anything. (It should be remembered that the only hard information anyone in Washington had at that point was James's first cable, and James himself had stressed in it that the picture in Korea was "still fragmentary" and "vague.") Some reporters went to State to see what they could get there. At 9:26 Muccio's telegram arrived, but the department's press officer, Lincoln White, told the press it would be a while before the cable was decoded—it was almost forty minutes. At 10:15 the decoding room sent a clear copy to White's office, where both Connors and White waited for it. They gave it to the reporters. A few minutes later Rusk came in, read the message, and immediately called Dean Acheson.

Acheson was spending the weekend at his Maryland

farm, about twenty miles north of Washington. The house, as Acheson described it, "was built in the nineteenth century and is very simple, very small, very quiet, and very secluded." But the secretary of state was never far from the hard, rough presence of reality. A special telephone (its bone-white color highly unusual at the time) linked him to the White House switchboard in case of emergency. Security guards moved quietly about his house, protecting him from possible assassination. All major public figures receive occasional hate mail; his had recently increased, no doubt due to McCarthy's attacks on him. (In early March a Manhattan astrologer-numerologist had studied Acheson's horoscope and suggested he had better "exercise extreme caution... during June, July, and August.") On that June 24, Acheson had gone to the farm about noon. He did some gardening, ate a good dinner, and settled into bed with a book. The white phone rang. [5]

Rusk read him Muccio's message and the two discussed it. Muccio, they agreed, was usually cautious and dependable; the situation in Korea was obviously "serious." But they decided they had better wait for more information. [6]

During the next hour Rusk phoned a number of other State Department officials from a list he apparently drew up on the spur of the moment. No record exists of all those he tried to contact, but by about midnight six of them arrived at State. The two most important were Jack Hickerson, assistant secretary for United Nations affairs, a careful civil servant from Texas, and Philip Jessup, a roving ambassador who had just completed a three-month tour of Asia, a man well known to be one of State's most enthusiastic supporters of the United Nations. Since the UN had a Commission on Korea and a team of observers there, Rusk's choice of Jessup and Hickerson (over all the potential people he might have called) seems logical. On the other hand, perhaps he was molding an "action team" that by its make-up would automatically turn to the UN for a solution. Rusk had, after all, been Hickerson's predecessor as the department's first assistant secretary for United Nations affairs. By 1950 respect for the UN among American leaders, never particularly high, had fallen off. (In his newspaper column James Reston said that, privately, neither Truman nor Acheson had much respect for the UN.[7] When Truman was asked much later if he would have been willing to go it alone in Korea without the UN, he replied, "No question about it."[8]) Probably Rusk on his own initiative was hoping to revitalize the organization. Or maybe he felt that working through the UN was not only "correct form" but might also offer a "cover" should the United States want to take more drastic, perhaps military, action.

Shortly after Hickerson arrived, he talked to Acheson on the phone. "What are your suggestions?" Acheson asked. Not surprisingly, Hickerson replied that he and Rusk (both UN specialists) agreed the United States should bring the matter before an emergency meeting of the UN Security Council and ask it to order both sides to stop fighting and return to their respective borders. Acheson concurred. He stipulated that they wait until he called Truman in Missouri to receive presidential approval. Meanwhile they should do two things: phone Trygve Lie, secretary general of the United Nations, to alert him they might shortly be asking him to call a Security Council meeting; and also keep in touch with the Pentagon. (Acheson mistakenly assumed that both Louis Johnson and Omar Bradley were still out of town, and given a growing rift between the two departments—to say nothing of a personal feud between himself and Johnson—he calculated it was best to stroke the Pentagon's ego.) The State Department men contacted Deputy Undersecretary of State Freeman Matthews, the liaison man with the Defense Department, and invited him to join them. They also invited Frank Pace, secretary of the army. Pace was a tall, good-looking young man, tanned from hours on golf courses and tennis courts around Washington, where he was a champion at both sports. He had a pleasant, friendly manner and thick black curly hair which he kept carefully brushed. He was the son of a well-to-do lawyer from Little Rock, Arkansas, and though a product of an Eastern prep school (The Hill) and of two Ivy League universities (Princeton and Harvard), he retained a trace of Arkansas twang. Before entering government service, he had been a hardworking, ambitious lawyer; he had been only twenty-seven when he argued his first case before the Supreme Court. He was appointed secretary of the army just a few months earlier and he had not yet solidified his position. He was a little insecure.

In Independence, Harry Truman had finished dinner and settled down in the living room to read. When the security phone rang, he went to the library to answer it.

"Mr. President," Acheson said, "I have serious news. The North Koreans are attacking across the thirty-eighth parallel."

Truman, man of action, wanted to return to Washington immediately but Acheson talked him out of it. The news from Korea was still garbled and there seemed no pressing reason yet to make a possibly dangerous night flight. Truman assented. Acheson then asked him about initiating action from the UN. Truman approved that too. Finally, the secretary of state asked if he could tell Frank Pace that Truman wanted the two departments to work together on this. Again, Truman agreed. The president then went to bed, but he later admitted, "That was one night I didn't get much sleep." In Maryland, carefully protected by whispering security guards, Acheson also tried to sleep.[9]

In Rome a small crowd of spectators gathered in St. Peter's Basilica to watch the pope perform a mass for Maria Goretti, beatified the day before. The Holy Father was late. Moments earlier, one of his foreign advisers had told him of events in Korea. He had entered his chapel to pray.[10]

Reporters continued to appear at the State Department. If war had really broken out in Korea, their editors thought, the situation might well be like Hitler's invasion of Poland, the first step toward world conflict. While such an eventuality appeared unlikely, journalistically it was always best to be sure. During the course of the evening, into the small hours, officials appeared in the pressroom to brief the waiting reporters.

John M. Chang, the ambassador from the Republic of Korea, also arrived at State. He remained all night. Syngman Rhee somehow reached him there and urged him to appeal to everyone within hearing—to the State Department, to the White House, and to the United Nations. At one point during the long night, Chang talked to reporters. "I don't think the United States will abandon us at all," he said, optimistically. [11]

As soon as Jack Hickerson hung up after talking to Acheson, he called Ernest Gross, acting chief of the American delegation to the UN. [12] (Warren Austin, the regular representative, was at his place in Rutland, Vermont, and was out of touch with events during the next twenty-four hours.) Ambassador Gross lived in Manhasset, on Long Island. That evening his teen-age daughter was giving a slumber party for a dozen or more girls. When Hickerson called, the girls were in their pajamas, no doubt giggling with overflowing pubescent adrenalin. No, Ambassador Gross was not there at the moment. He was at a dinner party somewhere. No, they did not know the telephone number where he could be reached.

Hickerson assured them the matter was urgent; when Ambassador Gross came in, would he please call the State Department immediately.

Hickerson then phoned Trygve Lie at his home in Forest Hills, Long Island. It was about midnight. Hickerson briefed him rapidly. Lie, a Norwegian, listened until Hickerson was finished, then said, "My God, Jack, this is war against the United Nations!"

"Trygve, you're telling me!" Hickerson replied.

Both men agreed the secretary general should do two things: find out where the other members of the Security Council were in case the United States decided to ask for a meeting right away; and send a cable to the UN Commission in Korea, asking it for any information it might have. (The commission's report arrived late that morning. It corroborated what was already known.)

Meanwhile, Ambassador Gross—somehow reached at his dinner party—contacted Hickerson, who told him to go home and await further word. Gross later recalled that when he reached his house, his daughter and her friends "were sprawled all over the living room, and I had to stagger over the recumbent bodies to get to the telephone."

"And," he remembers, "they clustered around the phone and began to get very excited. I imagine for them it was a memorable night, but they didn't get any more sleep than I did."

Gross made and received a dozen or more phone calls during the next few hours, talking to Lie, waking up other members of the Security Council and informing them of events in Korea. "They were all profoundly shocked by what had happened," Gross remembers. "They felt that the United Nations had to do something about it, that this was an attack on the UN itself."

While Gross on Long Island, surrounded by adolescent girls in bedroom attire, made his calls, in Washington the State Department prepared formal statements to be presented to the UN when it met that afternoon at two. At 8:30 A.M. two State Department officials hand-carried the formal drafts to New York in an army plane.

Almost simultaneously, a buzz of activity began at the UN. Preparations for the afternoon's session started shortly after dawn. By midmorning a stream of workers—guards, interpreters, electricians—bustled through the corridors. Secretaries laid out pencils and coffee cups; they made sure ash trays in the lounges were clean. The first diplomats arrived about one o'clock.

The Security Council met for almost four hours that afternoon. Speech followed speech in the tradition of international bodies. The resulting resolution, only slightly watered down from the statement written in Washington during the night, chastised North Korea for her "breach of the peace" and called upon her to "cease hostilities forthwith" and "to withdraw [her] armed forces to the 38th parallel."[13]

Compared to most diplomatic usage of the time, the resolution was reasonably hard-nosed. Its chief importance, however, was that it laid the groundwork for further UN steps. By labeling the opening rounds of this civil war a "breach of the peace," the Security Council had taken the stand that *peace* and the *status quo* were essentially the same. "Breach of the peace" is a legal phrase describing a crime. By using this phrase, the UN was declaring that any action which disturbed the political equilibrium (at least of the Western Powers or their client states) was *criminal* and its perpetrators were *outlaws*. This conclusion made later steps easier.

Throughout that Sunday morning, high-ranking military officials trickled into the Pentagon.

Matthew B. Ridgway, at the time deputy chief of staff of the army, recalls, "I was awakened by the tinkle of the telephone at my bedside and listened with growing uneasiness as the quiet, correct voice in midnight Washington told me of the message from Ambassador Muccio." Ridgway was in Pennsylvania but decided to return to his office at the Pentagon immediately. "I awakened my patient wife, to share my fears with her and to tell her to dress and to make ready to go right back to the capital." As they left their quarters, he was aware of "the country stillness" around him. "Long before the countryside was awake we were out on the dark road, talking very little."[14]

More than a hundred miles away, near the Maryland coast, Army Chief of Staff J. Lawton Collins woke to pounding at his front door. It was about five-thirty in the morning. At the door stood a sergeant. "General," he said, "the North Koreans have attacked, and you have to get to the Pentagon as fast as you can." Collins dressed, drank a quick cup of coffee, and left with the sergeant. "As we whirred north through the rolling tobacco fields of Maryland," he remembers, "my mind went back to another Sunday morning, when I heard over the radio word of the Japanese attack on Pearl Harbor."[15]

Omar Bradley (chairman of the Joint Chiefs), who had already been informed the night before, was awake when his aide called him at eight that morning with a report that the latest news from Korea was still insubstantial. Bradley left for his office.

By late morning the army had set up a special map room in the Pentagon and established a message center. Bradley and Secretary of Defense Louis Johnson waited, but the news from Korea was still vague, so they, along with Admiral Forrest Sherman, chief of naval operations, decided to follow their previously made plans to fly to Norfolk that afternoon for a public relations meeting with civilian business leaders. They were gone all afternoon. As a result, most of the decisions regarding Korea still remained in the hands of the State Department.

A conference began at State at eleven-thirty. Rusk, Hickerson, and Jessup were there. So were Pace and Collins and several other military men. Shortly past noon Acheson arrived. (A reporter for the *New York Herald Tribune*, haunting the State Department, hoping for developments, professionally attuned to subtle distinctions, noticed that when Acheson arrived he had his convertible top down and was in his shirt sleeves. Both facts were unusual, especially the latter. The secretary of state was normally an impeccable dresser. Presumably, thought the reporter, since the secretary was acting abnormally, he was feeling the tensions of the moment. Perhaps he was.)[16]

The conference at State went on for several hours. At 2:45 Acheson called the president.

The sky over Kansas City was clear but the air shimmered oppressively near ninety-seven humid degrees. Harry Truman left his house about eight o'clock that morning and drove to the family farm at Grandview, about twelve miles away. As a young man, he had plowed those fields; now his brother Vivian ran the farm. Truman, the ex-farmer, inspected a new milking machine and examined some horses. He chatted with Vivian and Vivian's children and grandchildren for about an hour and a half. He had planned to join them for a family luncheon but became skittish about Korea and left early. It was eleven-thirty when he got back to Independence.[17]

An hour or so later the phone rang. Margaret went to answer it. She came in and said, "Daddy, it's Dean Acheson, and he says it's important."

Truman later remembered, "I went to the phone and said, 'What is it, Dean?'

" 'Mr. President, the news is bad. The attack is in force all along the parallel.'

" 'Dean, we've got to stop the sons of bitches no matter what.' "[18]

He told Acheson to draw up a list of recommended actions and be prepared to present them to him that evening. He was returning to Washington immediately.

He ate a hurried lunch and drove to the airport with his wife and daughter. At the field a reporter from the *New York Times* thought Mrs. Truman seemed "calm but serious."

She looked, he said, the way she had that night back in 1945 when, with Roosevelt dead, Truman had taken the oath of office. Margaret, he noticed, stood off to the side, "staring up, absorbed, at her father's big plane, her hands clasped under her chin in a subconscious, prayerful attitude."[19]

As Truman was about to depart, he talked to reporters for a moment. "Don't make it alarmist," he said grimly, obviously feeling the weight of the moment, the responsibilities of his office. "It could be a dangerous situation but I hope it isn't. I can't answer any questions until I get all the facts." And he climbed into the plane.[20] Despite his own cautionary advice, he felt edgy and vaguely belligerent.

As the plane took off, an unnamed White House aide told reporters at the field, "The boss is going to hit those fellow hard."[21]

In her diary that night Margaret Truman jotted, "Everybody is extremely tense. Northern or Communist Korea is marching in on Southern Korea and *we are going to fight*."[22]

CHAPTER SIX

The First Blair House Conference

The finest hour in American history to date.

—Louis Johnson
(June 28, 1950)

It is a fundamental decision of American policy that the United States does not intend to permit further extension of Communist domination on the continent of Asia.

—Dean Acheson
(July 18, 1949)

WHILE HE WAS IN FLIGHT Truman contacted Acheson and told him to arrange a dinner conference at Blair House for later in the evening.

(Blair House was a yellow, stucco, four-story building at 1651 Pennsylvania Avenue. For months it had been Truman's official residence while workers rebuilt and refurbished the White House down the block. An attractive and generally tastefully furnished structure, Blair House had long been used to accommodate visiting dignitaries. When the floors of the White House began to sag noticeably,

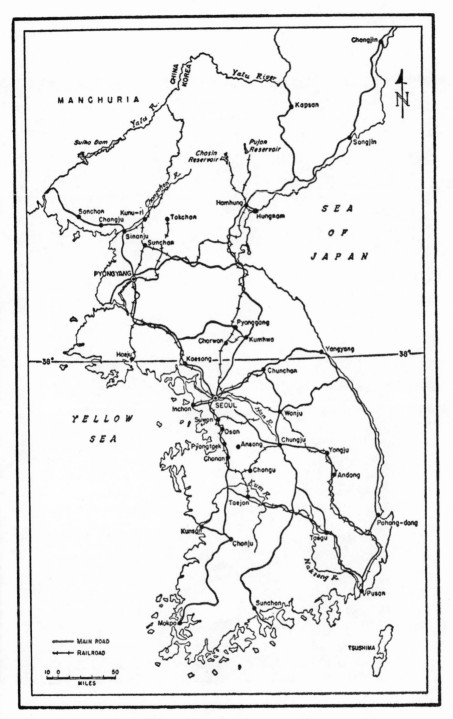

Korea. (United States Defense Department)

Harry S. Truman descends the gangplank of the presidential yacht *Williamsburg*. (Wide World Photos)

Blair House, November 1, 1950, the day two Puerto Rican nationalists tried to assassinate Truman. (John Zimmerman, TIME-LIFE Picture Agency,© Time Inc.)

The United Nations votes to enter the Korean War. (United Press International)

Truman, Louis Johnson (left), and Dean Acheson. (United Press International)

Refugees fleeing from the combat area near Taegu. (U. S. Army photo)

General MacArthur with Rear Admiral Austin K. Doyle behind. (Carl Mydans, TIME-LIFE Picture Agency,© Time Inc.)

U. S. ground troops arrive in Korea. (U. S. Army photo)

Truman and his family moved in here. The government erected two sentry boxes near the front door and placed a green canopy across the sidewalk from the curb to the entranceway.)

Late in the afternoon, Alonzo Fields received a phone call. Large, handsome, and black, Fields was the White House butler and presidential maître d'hôtel. He had served presidents since Herbert Hoover. On this Sunday he was told: "Fields, the President is flying back from Independence. He has invited the Chiefs of Staff, the Secretary of State and some others for dinner tonight. He is due at eight-thirty and the guests have been invited for eight o'clock. You are to have cocktails and hors d'oeuvres for them while they are waiting."[1]

Fields contacted two cooks and the three prepared a dinner and hors d'oeuvres for fourteen. Within a few hours they had a meal consisting of fruit cup, fried chicken, shoestring potatoes, buttered asparagus, scalloped tomatoes, hot biscuits, lettuce hearts with Russian dressing, vanilla ice cream with chocolate sauce, and coffee.[2] Before long, the shiny mahogany table in the small dining room reflected the lights of crystal chandeliers and polished silver, fine glassware and expensive linen.

The first guests arrived before eight. They waited in the drawing room, amidst the candy-striped sofas and floral-patterned rugs, while Alonzo Fields—the classic, efficient Washington butler—served them drinks. The group was tense. They gathered in small huddles and talked in hushed tones.

Meanwhile, Acheson, Louis Johnson, and Undersecretary of State James Webb waited at Washington National Airport for the president to land. Probably it was an awkward wait. Acheson and Johnson had been feuding for months. Both were ambitious, combative men. They genuinely, aggressively disliked each other.

Their styles conflicted.

Acheson, raised in an aristocratic, wealthy family, his father an Episcopalian bishop, his mother the heiress of a Canadian whiskey fortune, a graduate of Groton, Yale, and Harvard, was cerebral, lucid, and witty. A highly successful New York lawyer, he kept a tight rein on his temper. With his elegant dress, his cultivated manner, his carefully groomed mustache, and his vaguely clipped accent, he gave the appearance of a British diplomat. While he was pleasant and warm to those he liked and respected, he could be cold, aloof, condescending, and patronizing to those he did not. He liked to consider himself a jovial, personable fellow, well liked by the congressmen up on the Hill. He was not. He had a wealth of funny stories, but he lacked a common touch and made many people—including Louis Johnson—feel uncomfortable.

Johnson was born in Roanoke, Virginia, a grocer's son. In his teens he was a large, rawboned youth, fairly bright and extremely hardworking. He grew to about six three and weighed around two hundred pounds. He played football, won championships at boxing and wrestling, was the best student in his class, and was voted class president three times at the University of Virginia. He was an automatic choice for most-likely-to-succeed. In his twenties he became a lawyer and a Democratic politician. He married the richest girl in Clarksburg, Virginia. After service in World War I, where he won the Legion of Honor, he joined the American Legion, and of course rose right to the top. In two years he was its National Commander. He was also a president of the Rotary International, an Exalted Ruler of the Benevolent and Protective Order of Elks, a Mason, and a Son of the American Revolution. Truman chose him as secretary of defense.

The job of defense secretary brought with it immense pressures. James V. Forrestal was the first man to hold the office and he went mad. Before 1950 was out, Louis Johnson himself—ousted from the position—would be considered by a few to be somewhat unstable. The position seemed almost impossible. On the one hand came pressure to reduce expenditures; on the other, each of the services cried that it drastically needed money immediately or it could no longer guarantee protection to the country. By early 1950 all their voices were strident. Johnson, meanwhile, wanted to maintain or even cut the military budget. Many of the admirals and generals hated him.

As he and Acheson and Webb waited for Truman's plane to land, perhaps Johnson worried about his position in Truman's government. He and Acheson had each held their present positions for only a year and a half, and each vied with the other for Truman's ear. But it began to seem as if Acheson were winning the bureaucratic contest. While Johnson and Bradley had spent the day in Norfolk talking to civilians, Acheson had been the center of action. Johnson did not yet even know what suggestions the State Department had formulated that afternoon.

The men at State had spent the afternoon debating the alternatives. Their decisions helped to lay the foundation of America's Asian policies for the next generation. Much more than Korea was involved. But almost nothing is known about their discussions. They kept no accurate notes or minutes and their recollections are fuzzy. It is impossible to recreate their arguments with any absolute precision. But our knowledge of the participants, their assumptions, and their logic offer us some inkling of their thinking.

To understand why the United States entered a Korean civil war, one must place the situation in the context of American foreign policy. The ambitions and fears which motivated the United States in 1950 were extensions of old American inclinations.

The United States (or at least most of its business, military, and political leaders, who create its foreign policy) had always wanted to expand its trade; the prosperity of the nation demanded it. And prosperity, as the 1930s proved, affected almost everyone in the society. Any foreign country which threatened to reduce American trade, to close off its markets, was suspect; if that government was a military dictatorship, the combination of the two factors almost guaranteed the United States would openly oppose it. Dictatorships by themselves were repugnant to America's professed, and often practiced, beliefs in "decency" and political freedoms. But such despotisms were normally accepted, often with resignation, provided they allowed trade to run smoothly. A Latin American tyrant was just barely acceptable; an *expansionist* Nazi Germany, Japanese Empire, or Soviet Union was unacceptable.

After 1945 American leaders became concerned about the specter of social and political instability in the world. Many of them genuinely desired to aid the troubled and sick and starving—especially of those sections of Europe ethnically connected to our leaders (like England), or attached traditionally to our history (like France), or from which millions of voters came (like Italy, Greece, and even Germany). The United States recognized that there were other suffering peoples in the world but they seemed more remote, less part of our European "family." Neither ruthlessness nor crassness nor even racism made American leaders tend to overlook problems in Latin America, Africa, and most of Asia. They recognized a limit to America's ability to give aid. Since a choice had to be made, help would be given to those areas that were like "us" (that is, the leaders) and whose potential trade was more immediately significant. Better to aid the people of England than those of either Pakistan or Brazil. When the United States sent food or money to European countries like Italy, it hoped to stabilize the social and political climate there, to prevent a leftist takeover which might disrupt the international market.

Simultaneously, the American leadership hoped not only to control their international markets but to expand them. If

Britain collapsed in economic depression, that was bad—from a humanitarian point of view and for American trade. But if the British Empire began to crumble, that was not necessarily a total disaster, provided the result could be somewhat controlled. If Greece, for example, long an unofficial British protectorate, drew away from England, the United States might benefit. If Indonesia split from the Netherlands, American oil interests might gain. From 1945 to 1950 the United States slowly shouldered its way into the collapsing empires of the so-called European Great Powers, and she absorbed, as well, much of the position previously held by the Japanese Empire.

It seemed that the most immediate threat to both the market and the potential market was an amorphous political tendency, at times loosely managed and mismanaged by the Soviet Union, ponderously called by various pundits "International Communism." Exactly what this phrase meant was never clear. Partly it referred to the disruptive tendencies of leftist rebel leaders in sections of the decaying colonial world. Since economic radicals sometimes spurred themselves on by visions of Lenin and the Bolsheviks, and because the Kremlin occasionally sent representatives to encourage them, the radicals generally considered themselves, and were invariably called, Communists. (Marx would have been flabbergasted.) The rebel leftists irritated the United States because of their apparent connections to the USSR and because they caused turbulence in the marketplace.

So far as the United States was concerned, Stalinist Russia was a cowbird: Whatever nest it sat in became instantly tainted and repulsive. If the Kremlin supported a particular government, the United States was opposed.

Many reasons account for this attitude. Some of them, such as a generalized suspicion of radicals and an Anglo-Saxon distaste for Slavs, go deep into American history, long before the Russian Revolution. The Stalinist regime was recognized as narrow, totalitarian, and completely ruthless.

America had just fought the Nazis. There seemed a similarity between these two regimes. (Two goons standing on a corner may actually be quite different but still leave the same impression.)

The Soviet Union might not actually be aggressive toward the United States—and in retrospect it was not. American leaders might privately even admit that the Kremlin, within its crude, thuggish capabilities, was sometimes willing to appease the United States, in other words to back down. Truman and his advisers might even recognize that Russia was not behind every leftist revolt in the world. They certainly knew the Soviet Union was incapable of posing any threat to the United States. But they were willing to pretend that Russia was an immediate menace, or to convince themselves that it was. It was necessary, an aging senator once advised Truman, "to scare hell out of the American people."

Harry Truman personally did not like the Russian regime. (In fact, of course, the Kremlin was not at all likeable.) But Truman went beyond distaste; he purposely created the impression that Russia was an international bogeyman. It was not: Stalin was much too conservative and the Soviet Union was much too weak to serve as any threatening force outside Eastern Europe, an area which among other things served as Russia's bastion against Germany.

If the Soviets were not a menace why did Truman say they were? The answer is very complex and still shaded in doubt, but apparently at least part of the reason lay in Truman's (and Acheson's) belief that in order to avoid a devastating future war against anyone (a Third World War, as it was always called), the United States must make herself into an awesome power. Since the Soviet Union was the most likely, though not the only, candidate to threaten America in the future, and since she was a monstrous dictatorship anyway, she was a convenient scarecrow Truman could use to frighten Congress to pass the necessary (and expensive) military budgets. (To make matters even better, these appropriations, originally approved by Congress to set up air bases and loan money to friendly governments, could be used to stabilize the international marketplace.)

The idea of preventing war by being—or appearing—tough can be termed the Munich Theory of Aggression. America's leaders after 1939 had been impressed, probably overimpressed, with the argument that World War II could have been avoided by a show of strength earlier in the 1930s. For instance, that Hitler could have been stopped at the Munich discussions of 1938 had the British prime minister, Neville Chamberlain, rattled his battleships in Hitler's face. According to the theory, Hitler would have been awed by this exhibition, and therefore he would not have attacked Poland in September 1939 and begun the war. The appearance of weakness by Chamberlain at Munich, according to the theory, caused the war. As Dwight D. Eisenhower said just before the Korean War, "The pact of Munich was a more full blow to humanity than the atomic bomb at Hiroshima."[3]

The logic of this hypothesis seems to be that if a nation (or its leaders) indicates it is willing to fight, it does not have to. The unfortunate result of pursuing this policy too far is that it seems to reduce all diplomatic compromise to "appeasement." The Munich Theory consistently places one in the position of *appearing* implacable. But appearance is a psychological matter, having more to do with the attitude of one's opponent than it necessarily does with reality. Your foe must believe that you are capable and willing to fight. Your "prestige" becomes a crucial military matter. No wonder John F. Kennedy once asked whether prestige was "the shadow of power" or "the substance of power."

Important international areas therefore consist of the zones which are contested, for *it is only in a contest that one can display one's willingness to drive to the limit.* When Mao's

China took over Tibet or the large island of Hainan near the Gulf of Tonkin, that was unfortunate but acceptable. When Albania became communist, the reaction was the same. None of those areas was within a contested zone.

But when Greece or Cuba—or South Korea—was threatened, the entire question took on a different tone. As Acheson later said about America's reasons for entering the Korean War, the original attack seemed "an open, undisguised challenge to our internationally accepted position as the protector of South Korea." (No hypocritical nonsense here about how the United States was only aiding the United Nations.) Acheson went on: "To back away from this challenge, in view of our capacity for meeting it, would be highly destructive of the power and prestige of the United States. By prestige I mean the shadow cast by power, which is of great deterrent importance."[4]

Truman himself later claimed that while he was in the plane returning to Washington he mulled over the news from Korea. "If this was allowed to go unchallenged," he claimed he thought, "it would mean a third world war, just as similar incidents had brought on the second world war."[5]

Truman stewed about the possible international ramifications of this Korean incident. The next day he talked with one of his aides, George Elsey. The young man expressed concern about how Korea might affect China. Elsey recalls clearly what happened then: "The President walked over to the globe standing in front of the fireplace and said he was more worried about other parts of the world . . . What he was worried about, the President said, was the Middle East. He put his finger on Iran and said: 'Here is where they will start trouble if we aren't careful.'"

Truman continued, "Korea is the Greece of the Far East. If we are tough enough now, if we stand up to them like we did in Greece three years ago, they won't take any next steps." (Note the assumption that there is one unified, monolithic "they." Russia, Greece, Korea, all were interlocked, in Truman's mind, as if they had a single motivating force, an interconnected nervous system. Tickle them in one crevice, they will wriggle all over.) "But if we stand by," he continued, "they'll move into Iran and they'll take over the whole Middle East. There's no telling what they'll do if we don't put up a fight now."[6]

Nor were Truman and Acheson alone in their conclusions. Congressional leaders during the next few days voiced identical sentiments.[7] And John Foster Dulles' immediate reaction was the same. As soon as he heard about Korea, he wired the State Department: "To sit by while Korea is overrun by unprovoked armed attack would start [a] disastrous chain of events leading most probably to world war."[8]

Yet Korea was *not* strategically important. America's military leadership had long advised the government to sever ties with Rhee's regime and accept the possibility of a Communist takeover. In early 1948 the Joint Chiefs of Staff sent a recommendation to Harry Truman which stated in part: "The United States should not become so irrevocably involved in the Korean situation that an action taken by any faction in Korea [the Democratic People's Republic] or by any other power in Korea [the Soviet Union] could be considered a 'casus belli' for the United States." The following year the Joint Chiefs reiterated their position. The National Security Council and the president, moreover, confirmed the decision.[9]

On July 12, 1949, the Foreign Relations Committee of the Senate held secret hearings. It invited Major General W. E. Todd, intelligence specialist for the Joint Chiefs, to talk to them about Korea. Henry Cabot Lodge asked him a question.

LODGE: "If the Russians did take Korea, would they have strengthened themselves very much?"

TODD: "No sir, the Soviets in Sakhalin, eastern Siberia, and Vladivostok, are in as favorable [a] position as they would be if they took the rest of Korea."

LODGE: "It is not to be presumed that the reasons the Soviets give South Korea such a low priority that to take it would mean a sacrifice?"

TODD: "It is a liability."

LODGE: "So if we did let the Soviets take Korea, looking at it cold-bloodedly, what harm would it do to us?"

TODD: "From my standpoint it has practically no strategic significance."

Senator Walter F. George of Georgia interrupted to ask a question, fascinating in light of later discussions: "Would it have [strategic significance] with reference to Japan?" Many of the later arguments in favor of America's intervention in Korea would be based upon the oft-stated premise that Korea was a "dagger at the heart of Japan." If it "fell," the theory said, Japan would be threatened. This early domino thesis was based presumably on a belief that geopolitical changes are as contagious as cold germs (or worse, are like medieval plagues, which ignorant peasants believed floated in the air from village to village).

Todd's reply to Senator George was: "No, sir, Japan is almost under the guns of Mukden, Sakhalin, and the Kurils. The Russians would be a little closer across the Tsushima Strait, but the gain for the Soviet Union would be small, we feel—very small indeed."

When asked if General MacArthur agreed, Todd said, "He was most anxious for us to withdraw our occupation forces there, Senator. He has been, all along. He has regarded it as of no importance from a military standpoint."[10]

The military was aware that either the Soviet Union or North Korea might attack after American troops left. In January 1948, *before* the Joint Chiefs first suggested the United States withdraw her forces from Korea, the Joint Strategic Survey Committee considered the potential results of such an action and sent its conclusions to the Joint Chiefs. Its report stated that "eventual domination of Korea by the USSR will have to be accepted as a probability if U.S. troops are withdrawn."[11]

It is clear that the army had written off Korea and had attempted to put it out of the "contested zone." The president, the secretary of state, the Joint Chiefs, and the National Security Council had all agreed—with greater or lesser enthusiasm—that Korea was indeed "outside our defense perimeter." What, then, was different by June 1950 to cause all this reaction?

Three factors.

First, the reality of an assault on South Korea was different than the theory. One might philosophize academically in 1948 about such an attack and suggest it ought to have no effect. Many things work in theory and not in practice.

Second, the individuals leading the discussions in 1950 were not from the military arm of the government, but worked out of the State Department. And State had always been hawkish on Korea. While the men at State did not particularly care about that Asian nation, they saw it as a "negotiating chip" in the American-Soviet rivalry over China and Japan.[12] It was State that had pressed for a military advisory team for South Korea. Muccio's huge establishment in Seoul resulted from State's attitude about Korea. Because of the State Department's concern, and the men and women it sent to Seoul, Korea had become a "commitment." Whether or not the military liked it, Korea was part of America's sphere of influence—and thus *was* within the contested zone.

Third, many new elements had entered the picture after the summer of 1949, after General Todd told the Senate Foreign Relations Committee that Korea was a "liability."

In September 1949 Truman announced that Russia had just set off an atomic device. Physicists had long advised that Russia would soon have nuclear weapons, but most people had apparently preferred to ignore their warnings. Russia's nuclear success, therefore, although it should not have done so, startled Truman. No longer did America have a monopoly on the Ultimate Weapon. While certainly the United States was still far ahead in nuclear capacity, she now had to peer constantly over her shoulder.

This new arms race was in itself tensive; the implications of a vast nuclear war came home to Americans. Schoolchildren learned what to do in case of atomic attack: Huddle on the floor and cover your face and hands. *Time* reported that officials in Chicago were prepared to tattoo each citizen's blood type beneath his or her armpit—in case all four arms and legs were blown off. Ads for real estate in the Washington, D.C., area now proclaimed it was "out beyond atom bombs" or "a safe 58 miles from Washington" or "out of the radiation zone." Just four days before the Korean War began, Congressman John McCormack of Massachusetts, accompanied by Governor Paul Dever, asked Harry Truman to help Boston build an atom bomb–proof parking garage.[13]

Truman also reacted—especially when told the Russians were accelerating their atomic pace and should soon develop thermonuclear power—H-bomb capacity. Throughout the winter of 1949–1950 officials of the State Department and various military and intelligence services held highly secret meetings. They pondered America's strength and international position relative to the Soviet Union and its allies. In early April they handed the president their conclusions. Truman turned the report over to the National Security Council to consider its ramifications. The NSC thought deeply about it and in late April arrived at its conclusions. Its paper was called NSC-68. It is still secret.

Its profile, however, has gradually materialized. It called for a huge increase in America's military commitments. It suggested a doubling or tripling of the country's military forces. And it proposed stepped-up military aid to allies and potential allies. If the suggestions were followed, it would mean gigantic military and foreign aid budgets. These might be difficult to maneuver through a financially conservative Congress.

There is no way of knowing if NSC-68 played any part in the State-Defense discussions of June 25 or the following few days. By itself probably not. But the assumption that the United States must strengthen herself (and her allies) underlay the debate. There is no evidence that the report itself guided the discussion that week, but the attitudes which created it two months earlier were still there.

Another factor in America's international posture since 1948 was the situation in Asia. Chiang Kai-shek had fallen. Mao Tse-tung announced the creation of the People's Republic of China on October 1, 1949. During the next few months he solidified his position, took Tibet and the island of Hainan, and prepared for an invasion of Formosa.

Elsewhere in Asia much was happening. In the poorer farm areas north of Manila an underground leftist group called the Hukbalahaps (Huks) made trouble for the Philippine government. Meanwhile, the old European colonies in Asia were collapsing—Malaya, Indonesia, Burma. In Indochina Ho Chi Minh's guerrillas cut roads, made bombs, and generally harassed the French. (America's motives in Indochina were complex: possibly a desire for expanded trade at the expense of the French; certainly a distaste for radicals in general and Communists in particular; most of all, given the European focus of American foreign policy at the time, her foreign aid to France was meant to buttress a moderately conservative regime in Paris and an anti-Soviet France in Europe.)

In 1949 the United States began to tighten its position in Asia. As Philip Jessup, one of State's most prestigious thinkers, later asserted, the department wanted to bring its Asian strategy "in line with the containment policy." Jessup admits that State worried about its pallid reputation. "We had to act with a real sense of theater to cater to people's imagination." By mid-1949 State's planning agency was writing muscular memorandums about how to strengthen America's posture throughout the Asian continent, including the Philippines, Japan, and India. On July 18, 1949, Acheson sent Jessup a note which began, "You will please take as your assumption that it is a fundamental decision of American policy that the United States does not intend to permit further extension of Communist domination on the continent of Asia or in the southeast Asia area." [14]

The Japanese situation also seemed very complicated. Now that Chiang had collapsed, unless the United States could deal immediately with Mao, which appeared increasingly unlikely, Japan would have to become America's bastion in Asia. The State Department began to formulate a treaty with Japan, officially terminating World War II and ending the occupation. (That was the reason John Foster Dulles was in Japan, to discuss a preliminary draft.)

When the State Department dealt with Japan, it confronted more than the Japanese—it faced Douglas MacArthur. Lately he had been displeased. He was very concerned about Chiang Kai-shek. He recognized that Truman's government had decided to allow Formosa to fall to Mao, and he thought it a serious mistake. He presented this conclusion to everyone who would listen. Officials, making the Pacific tour, received the MacArthur treatment. Most recently this had included Louis Johnson and Omar Bradley. When they returned to Washington from Tokyo they brought with them a formal expression of MacArthur's views. Johnson was anxious to show it to Truman—and perhaps the press. (Johnson, however, was not one of MacArthur's puppets. At the first Blair House conference on Korea, Johnson would advise Truman not to give MacArthur too much discretion, not to delegate too much authority to the proud general in Tokyo. [15]) Johnson may have seen MacArthur's disgruntlement over Truman's China policy as a weapon he could use in his bureaucratic struggle with Acheson.

Another, if unspoken, part of the diplomatic equation on

June 25 was politics. Truman was unpopular and the State Department was in great disfavor. "Public approval" polls on the president revealed a residual distaste for him. In January 1949, at the beginning of his first elected term, 69 percent approved of his leadership. One year later the figure had dropped to 45 percent. By June 1950 it stood at 37 percent.[16] Children, seeing their president on movie newsreels, threw popcorn at the screen while adults in the audience laughed. In fact almost the only time Truman ever achieved much approval during his eight years in office was when he took belligerent stands—against Communist guerrillas in Greece, or the Russians in Berlin, or that "no-account, do-nothing, Re-publican, Eightieth Congress." Give-'em-hell Harry gained affection. It was as though the polls preferred Mr. Hyde to Dr. Jekyll. Such a thing could encourage a peaceful man to drink the potion.

Some Republicans had long made the charge that Democrats in general and Truman in particular were soft on communism. Countless revelations in the period from 1948 to 1950, including the famous ones about ex–New Dealer Alger Hiss, seemed to affirm this suspicion. But few were willing to finger any high-ranking Democrat *still* in office. Until Joe McCarthy. Beginning in February, the senator from Wisconsin gained headlines by simply stating that he had damaging evidence against specific individuals in the government—particularly in the State Department and especially in that section of it primarily concerned with America's confused Asian policies. Democratic leaders were sure McCarthy had nothing. They agreed among themselves to destroy him by suggesting he provide Congress with his "valuable evidence." Senate hearings took place. McCarthy and his Democratic foes fenced for weeks over this name or that, throughout March and April 1950. McCarthy challenged the State Department's abilities and the loyalties of its members. The echoes still reverberated two months later when the Korean War broke out.[17]

There is no evidence that on June 25, in formulating its

suggestions for Truman, the State Department officials considered either the politics of the Democratic party or their own damaged, sissified reputations. But men's motives are complex. Decisions result from a morass of conscious and unconscious desires. Some, like a defense of democracy, may be philosophical. Others may be motivated by ethnic prejudice, religious inclinations, political ambitions, or bureaucratic infighting. Still others go deeper, far deeper within the psyches of decision makers, to the stuff of Freudian or Jungian nightmares. ("Mr. President, was you popular when you was a boy?" "Why, no . . . to tell the truth I was kind of a sissy.")

On the afternoon of June 25, as Truman was flying in from Missouri, the men of the State Department were under pressure to arrive at intelligent suggestions. But first they had to ask themselves a series of specific questions.

Was the fighting in Korea merely a civil war? Were the North Koreans acting at the behest of the Russians? Was it a test of wills?

The State Department group concluded immediately, apparently without real discussion and with paltry evidence, that Russians had initiated the attack; it was not a simple civil war.

Was it a feint? Did the Russians hope to draw the United States into an Asian maelstrom while the real action took place elsewhere? Could it be Iran? Or Turkey? Two days earlier Bulgarian troops had been reported moving toward the border of Yugoslavia. Just as the Korean War began, Bulgaria suddenly protested about Turkish military activity along their common border. [18] How about Berlin?

The men at State were unsure whether Korea was the signal for a generalized world assault. They did not want the United States to become irrevocably bogged down there, in case the real action was going to take place somewhere else.

What did Intelligence have to say? For that matter, why hadn't Intelligence warned them of North Korea's attack?

Part of the problem with America's intelligence gathering was the byzantine workings of the bureaucracy that ran the spy system. The United States government had indeed received a number of accurate warnings of the assault. But evidence of an attack is insufficient by itself. The government receives continual warnings of attacks from everywhere. On a given day, if data alone were to be believed, the United States would no doubt be under bombardment by the forces of Albania, Upper Volta, or Mars. It is up to Intelligence to *evaluate* the information—reject most, look for corroborating evidence for some, believe a very little. As far as Korea is concerned, Intelligence had not digested the raw information but had just sent all the rumors along. Clearly, American Intelligence failed in Korea. A shakeup within America's spy community lasting for months would later result.[19]

Another problem the conferees at State had to examine was America's military *capability* of reacting. They concluded that of all the disputed areas in the world, Korea was the most convenient place for the use of American military might. The Seventh Fleet was in the Philippines, the air force was concentrated on Okinawa and in Japan, and MacArthur had at his disposal four divisions which had just completed field maneuvers a few weeks earlier. South Korea, moreover, had usable airfields and port facilities. While United States military units in Asia were understrength, underarmed, and less well trained than they might be, all they would probably have to face were a few divisions of North Koreans. If it came to that, the Pentagon was not too concerned.[20]

What about American civilians in South Korea? The conferees discussed several alternative methods of evacuating them.

Finally, they analyzed the implications Korea had for the

rest of Asia. If South Korea fell, would this not encourage Ho Chi Minh? And the Huks? What about Chiang Kai-shek? They were concerned but came to no immediate conclusions.

After participating for several hours in these discussions, after listening to the welter of questions, Dean Acheson withdrew to his office—and cogitated. "During the afternoon I had everyone and all messages kept out of my room for an hour or two while I ruminated about the situation."[21] He made no long-range decisions; the proposals he decided on were merely measures to carry the matter through the next day or so. Too many unanswered questions still remained. Perhaps by tomorrow, or the day after, the direction of events in Korea would become clearer.

He drew up the following recommendations: (1) MacArthur should send supplies to Korea immediately. (2) Air cover should be used to protect the evacuation of American civilians. (3) If North Korean tanks or planes interfered with the evacuation, American pilots should destroy them. (4) A study should be made of what other type of aid might be provided under UN auspices. (5) The Seventh Fleet should proceed to Formosa to prevent an attack by either side upon the other. While on the one hand Acheson believed the United States "should not tie up with the Generalissimo" (Chiang Kai-shek), he felt that at the moment it would be best to avoid having the Asian picture become more complicated. Possibly the whole problem might be solved by the UN. (6) America should increase its aid to Indochina.[22]

Before he left for the airport to meet Truman, Acheson had one last conference at State to talk over his list of suggestions. No one disagreed with any of them.[23]

Shortly before eight Truman arrived at Blair House accompanied by Acheson, Johnson, and Undersecretary Webb. Before he did anything else, the president withdrew for a few moments and called his wife to tell her he was safe.[24] He then joined the others. Thus began the first Blair House conference, whose discussions would eventually involve the United States in a war.

The room glittered with fourteen of the highest-ranking members of the State Department and the military. Truman sat on a window seat at the side. Acheson told the whole group briefly what had happened that afternoon at the UN. Then, as they still waited for dinner to be announced, Louis Johnson asked Omar Bradley to read MacArthur's memorandum on the importance of Formosa. While the others sipped their cocktails, Bradley read it without interruption. Before anyone could comment Truman said, "We will put off all discussion of everything until we have had our dinner and then get things cleared away."[25] Alonzo Fields came in and told them dinner was ready.

As they entered the dining room, Undersecretary Webb drew Truman aside for a moment. While everyone might seem in agreement about Korea, Webb said, "Let's not do it too fast."

"Don't worry, I won't," Truman replied.[26]

(One wonders what Webb meant by his cryptic warning. What difficulty did he sense? He had stood at the airport with Johnson and Acheson. Had anything been said there? It is an interesting riddle.)

For the next few minutes the conferees concentrated on the meal Fields and the cooks had prepared. While black servants noiselessly glided in and out, as unobtrusively as always, the generals and diplomats solemnly masticated their chicken and biscuits, their ice cream with chocolate sauce.

After the dishes were cleared and the servants gone, the men remained where they were seated around the long mahogany table. And the conference began.

Acheson opened with his list of recommendations. When he finished, the first to reply was Omar Bradley, who de-

clared that "we must draw the line somewhere."[27] Truman
agreed. Bradley suggested the United States "act under the
guise of aid to the United Nations." (Note the word "guise";
note also that no one objected.) Bradley also "questioned the
advisability of sending in ground troops." Secretary of the
Army Frank Pace and Secretary of Defense Louis Johnson
absolutely agreed on this point. At the very beginning,
therefore, those who spoke for the army were opposed to
committing infantry.

General Hoyt S. Vandenberg of the air force cautioned
them that Russian planes based in places like Shanghai
might threaten any action America might take in Korea.
Truman asked whether the United States could "knock out
their bases in the Far East." Vandenberg replied that "it
could be done if we used A-bombs." The implications were
clear: If the Russians entered the war, even with only their
planes, Truman and his government might well use nuclear
weapons. But it did not seem likely to come to that. Both
Bradley and Admiral Forrest Sherman agreed that Russia
"is not yet ready for war."

The conferees suggested that MacArthur should send a
survey team to Korea to provide accurate, first-hand information about the war.

Truman had listened to his advisers; now he gave out his
orders. He went beyond Acheson's proposals.

(1) MacArthur was to send military supplies to Korea.

(2) He was also to send a survey team.

(3) The Seventh Fleet should prepare to leave the
Philippines and steam toward Japan. (Everyone there understood that the ships would actually move to the Formosa
Strait, but they considered the Korean situation so inchoate
that it might be premature to give orders sending the fleet
directly to Formosa. Better it should prepare to go "toward
Japan.") Meanwhile, part of the Pacific Fleet in California
should move to Pearl Harbor.

(4) A broad and careful analysis should be made of the

"next probable place in which Soviet action might take place." (Truman assumed that Korea was the opening gun of a new phase of the cold war. He believed Russia had suddenly become aggressive. From this moment on, for the rest of his administration, Truman would react with almost ruthless ferocity to any sign of further Soviet "aggression."[28])

(5) "The Air Force should prepare plans to wipe out all Soviet air bases in the Far East." He emphasized this was merely an order that they should make *plans,* not attack.

(6) He authorized American planes to destroy North Korean tanks, "if necessary." Superficially, this meant they were to cover the evacuation. The young pilots who were given this order followed it precisely. They did not search out Korean tanks. (Acheson was displeased. "We had hoped, and rather indicated," he later said, apparently meaning himself and the State Department members who had drawn up the original recommendations, "that in doing this, they [the pilots] would not be too careful about just meeting planes that came over the airfields—if they saw any North Korean planes anywhere in the neighborhood, they were to go after them and get them out of the way." Acheson uses here a marvelous set of euphemisms. How could the pilots see planes "in the neighborhood" unless they went looking for them; and for that matter, what was "the neighborhood"? Acheson's expression "get them out of the way" should be read as "shoot them down, kill them." His language, even four years later, spotlights an existential fact: Bureaucratic phraseology—"surgical bombing," "megadeaths"—allows military decision-making to remain aloof from reality. In 1950 Acheson was convinced that the military mind was not bellicose enough. The failure of pilots to search and destroy "became somewhat of a disappointment, because General Bradley did not want to put that explicitly in the orders—saying that the lieutenants who flew these planes could be depended upon to interpret their

instruction broadly." Thus were born situations like those in Vietnam where low-ranking officers went beyond the explicit directions and followed the obvious *meaning* of the orders. Acheson later admitted he was "disappointed" because the pilots followed their orders precisely. "In fact, they didn't interpret them broadly, and therefore since there were no attacks on the airports as such, they didn't look for any trouble beyond that area." Ironically, one year later he and Truman would fire MacArthur partly for interpreting orders "broadly."[29]

Truman's decisions were aggressive, almost warlike. He had not pushed any buttons; but he had made sure they were in working order, and he—and his advisers—had made a genuine *psychological commitment* to military action. Acheson later reminisced: "It was an interesting discussion, because as I recall it the assumption by everybody—I don't think there was a question in anyone's mind or that it entered into the discussion that took place—as to whether we would or would not stand up . . . I think it was just sort of clear to us, almost without discussion, that we were going to."[30]

By his decision to send planes into combat, Truman had placed one foot into the rushing river of war hoping to stop the flow. If this did not succeed, it would seem only logical to step in with the other foot. He was prepared to give 'em hell.

The conference was over. Its participants would probably meet again tomorrow night. Truman emphasized they all must keep everything mentioned here to themselves. He himself would make some announcement to the press on Tuesday. Meanwhile, he wanted no leaks. James Webb suggested they might discuss the political ramifications, but Truman snapped, "I'll handle the political affairs."[31] The conferees slipped quietly out the back, while the president's press secretary told newsmen waiting out front that Truman had no comment as yet.

In Tokyo, meanwhile, MacArthur's headquarters staff, reading over some of Acheson's recommended actions, said, "Come over and join the fight. We are delighted with your lines of actions and this aid should turn the trick. Thank you."[32]

CHAPTER SEVEN

Momentous
Decisions

I don't want to go to war.
—Harry S. Truman
(June 27, 1950)

When whales fight, the shrimp are eaten.
—Ancient Korean proverb

SUNDAY MORNING WAS lovely in Tokyo. The sky shone crystal blue for the first time in weeks. Later in the day, as the temperature and humidity climbed toward the nineties, the Japanese fled the city for the beaches and picnic areas.

About midmorning, Muccio's first report arrived at MacArthur's headquarters in Tokyo. Three hours passed until his staff at the Dai Ichi Building concluded that the North Koreans had attacked in force, before they were willing to phone MacArthur and disturb him in his bedroom at the embassy.[1] ("I remember being told," Dean Acheson later reminisced, "that they didn't dare to wake him up to tell him the attack had occurred, so there was some delay in getting the message to him."[2]) When told, MacArthur was unconcerned. The day was beautiful. There had been many such incidents along the Korean border. Several hours later he had an interview with a reporter; he did not even mention Korea. In fact he told the journalist that he did not think there would be any war in Asia in the foreseeable future. He talked mostly of Japan, of Russia, and of "those asses back in Washington."[3]

Americans in Tokyo became aware of the fighting during the afternoon. Radio Tokyo carried the stories, alternating music and grim bulletins. John M. Allison, a State Department official temporarily in Japan with John Foster Dulles, recalls how he first heard of it. He had been to a friend's for lunch and returned to his hotel about three. "As I walked through the lobby to my room, I was hailed by two other friends, former Japanese Ambassador to Washington Horinochi and Harry Kearn, Foreign News Editor of *Newsweek*, who were having tea."

"Have you heard about the war in Korea?" they asked.

"What war?" he replied.

They told him.[4]

Allison rushed to his room and began to make telephone calls. One of MacArthur's aides informed him that William Sebald, the State Department's liaison man with MacArthur's headquarters, and John Foster Dulles had both been notified. MacArthur expected to see Dulles, Sebald, and Allison at the Dai Ichi Building at six o'clock.

That evening MacArthur was buoyant with optimism and, as usual, absolutely impressive. "General MacArthur," Allison remembers, "was magnificent as he strode up and down his huge office, his khaki shirt open at the neck, and his famous corncob pipe gripped between his teeth."

"This," MacArthur said about the attack in Korea, "is probably only a reconnaissance in force. If Washington will not hobble me, I can handle it with one arm tied behind my back." (He was still more concerned with those "asses back in Washington.") He said everything was under control. "This really probably isn't serious." He also told them that he had begun the process of sending munitions. (The ship carrying them would not arrive in Korea until June 28.

Supplies would not reach ROK units until June 29, by which time most Korean units were in headlong retreat.)

As soon as Dulles, Sebald, and Allison left MacArthur's office after the meeting, a newsman from the United States named William Mathews entered. "MacArthur was very calm," Mathews recalls.

"I hope the American people have the guts to rise to meet this situation," the general said. "I know they have it in them. . . . The next 48 hours will tell whether the South can hold. I believe it will hold."

All at once MacArthur changed the subject and started to talk about politics. He asked Mathews, "What about American politics? Who will win in November?" Then, later, "What about 1952?" The newsman told him of Robert Taft's campaign and of the growing swell for Eisenhower. MacArthur "eulogized Taft" and asserted that Eisenhower would ruin the Republican party. The party, he insisted, should not compromise its principles just to win an election.

"I am ready to serve at any time," he said, "in any capacity, anywhere."[5]

While the general was pontificating about politics in his office, Dulles and Allison sat in Dulles' guest quarters at the embassy talking about Korea. Dulles felt a sense of personal responsibility for the Korean regime. He had just returned from Seoul, where he had told its National Assembly: "You are not alone. You will never be alone as long as you continue to play worthily your part in the great design of human freedom."

Dulles and Allison agreed that MacArthur was possibly too optimistic. They wondered whether recent secret discussions between Mao and Stalin had instigated the attack. They worried it might be only the first step toward an eventual takeover of Japan. Dulles took out a legal pad of yellow-lined paper, and the two men drafted a message for Acheson and Rusk. They stated they hoped South Korea could contain the assault; if not, they suggested "United States force." Otherwise, "to sit by while Korea is overrun by unprovoked armed attack would start a disastrous chain of events leading most probably to world war."

Despite a few war jitters most Americans in Japan relaxed that Sunday night. A few officers at headquarters answered jangling phones and anxiously followed the course of battle using pins on wall maps, but most occupation troops went through their normal routine: movies, drinking, cards, sex. Northwest Airlines was still taking commercial bookings to Seoul for later in the week.[6]

By Monday things seemed even calmer. General William F. Dean, stationed south of Toyko (and soon to be a prisoner of the North Koreans), remembers: "On June 26 we had new information from Korea: the South Korean Army was counterattacking and the situation looked much better than it had the day before.

"We had several South Korean officers on a tour of duty with our division," Dean continued, "and I began to worry about them. But when I sent a message to Tokyo, asking whether we should get them back to Korea right away, I was told, 'No. Have them finish their courses, and prepare to receive another group in July.'" In other words, business as usual. "This was going to be a short and easy war."[7]

During the morning Dulles and Allison dropped by MacArthur's office. They found the general still confident. "Again the General was most impressive and most cordial," Allison recalls. "Well," the general said, "the fighting's a little more severe but we can still handle it all right." (Notice the interesting collective pronoun "we," referring to the South Koreans. What might happen if "we" began to lose?) MacArthur told them that Muccio was evacuating American women and children. Personally, he said, he thought Muccio was premature, that he had become "panicky."[8]

In Korea John Muccio prepared to evacuate approximately seven hundred dependents (women and children) connected to AMIK. He had been worried about their fate, and he wanted them out of Korea so he could concentrate on other things. For a year the embassy had had an evacuation plan called Operation Cruller. Depending on such circumstances as weather, availability of transportation, and the attack itself, Americans and certain designated non-Americans would be sped out of danger.[9]

Muccio told Jack Seifert, naval attaché at the embassy, to check what ships might be available to take passengers out of Korea. Seifert called the harbor facilities in nearby Inchon. Two ships were available: the S.S. *Reinholt,* a Norwegian freighter, and the S.S. *Norge,* a Nationalist Chinese ship. Both captains said they would be willing to sail for Japan.

About midnight Sunday the armed forces radio station in Seoul, WVTP, announced that all dependent women and children should be at the motor pool by three that morning. Each person could only bring one small bag. Each should carry a blanket.

A telephone relay system began and phones rang all over Seoul. Friends contacted friends. Messengers ferreted out others.

By three, buses started to leave the city. For the dependents it was the beginning of a harrowing experience. Many were frightened, some had calmed their nerves with drink. A few were drunk. Throughout the night women cried in the blackness or swore at one another. Muffled sobs punctuated the bus rides, and the quiet sniveling of tired babies awakened in the middle of the night to stand or sit in the dark while strangers shoved them and shouted. The sun was rising as the first buses arrived at Inchon.

During the next day or so, some adults also cracked. An observer recalls: "One married couple broke down and had to be carried out in improvised strait jackets."[10]

When the women stood on the dock gazing at the two ships, most felt an understandable stab of anxiety. The Norwegian freighter had been carrying a cargo of fertilizer. The fertilizer was gone now but the odors lingered on. Moreover, the ship was only supposed to have room for twelve passengers. Its hold and deck had been cleared for an overload, but not for seven hundred people. The Chinese vessel seemed worse. According to one account, "the women were so terrified at the thought of boarding a Chinese ship, which to their tortured minds might take them any place except to safety, especially as they approached the vessel and saw the curious Chinese crew peering down at them from high above, that every single one of them refused to go aboard."[11] Perhaps it was the yellow skins or the epicanthic folds which slanted their eyes; those were *orientals* on that ship, like the devils who were coming south toward Seoul. The official government document on this incident says, more diplomatically (and possibly more accurately), that the Chinese ship was too filthy to use at the time.[12] All seven hundred women and children boarded the Norwegian *Reinholt* and packed themselves in. The ship did not sail until almost four-thirty in the afternoon. Many evacuees had been awake for almost thirty-six hours. They sat or lay amidst the stink of fertilizer, soon mixed with the sour smell of vomit. The motionless, fetid air of the holds heated up, warmed by hundreds of sweaty bodies packed together. The outside air was in the nineties, heavy and humid. Inside was a nightmare. Some became hysterical.

They remained on the *Reinholt* three days. It was a name they would remember.

Fifty of them had to be taken off the ship by stretcher. Three women had false labor. One child had smallpox. Thirty children had dysentery.

Yet the seven hundred were lucky. Had a severe storm risen while they were at sea, the results might have been catastrophic. As it was, no one died. Muccio could state that the evacuation had taken place without even a bloody nose.[13]

The seven hundred may not have felt quite so fortunate, however, when in Japan they discovered many friends from AMIK they had left behind in Seoul who had flown over painlessly while the *Reinholt* was still at sea. By Monday night Muccio had decided to send out all those female staff members who had refused to leave earlier, plus most of the male staff. He also offered to send out all the missionaries, all the French and British subjects, and the staffs of the UN and Chiang Kai-shek's embassy. By dawn Tuesday, while the *Reinholt* was still in the Yellow Sea, six transport planes began evacuation shuttle flights from Korea.

Eventually, by one means or another, more than 2,000 westerners arrived in Japan, more than 1,500 of them Americans. Many staggered into reception centers exhausted and in confusion, anxiously peering around for wives or husbands. As they stood in long slow lines or at registration tables, they often carried odd assortments of paraphernalia, as if they had not been able to decide what to bring, what was important. Many men toted shotguns they had originally taken with them to Kimpo airfield in case guerrillas attacked before they took off. One lady tightly held a cocker spaniel; another had two antique vases. (One man later remembered that before he left Seoul he worried what to take; he finally decided to bring a wooden Chinese sculpture a friend had left with him.) Over at the side, like a cameo scene from a movie, two soldiers in the midst of the bustle tried fumblingly in their high school French to aid a Swiss nun.

Some of those invited to evacuate did not leave. The British minister, Vyvyan Holt, elected to stay. So did the French chargé d'affaires; so did a Catholic bishop and a French journalist. An ECA official returned to Seoul that Tuesday after a long jeep ride. He knew no Korean. He did not know that AMIK was gone. Exhausted, he went straight to bed in his hotel room. He disappeared when the North Koreans took the city. An American financial expert, attached to AMIK, had not felt well the last few weeks. He had entered a hospital for observation just before the war began. His fever rose; the doctors diagnosed his illness as polio. As the last evacuation buses left Seoul, he died, alone. Two Korean doctors came to the embassy to ask the leaving Americans what to do with the body. No one at the embassy had an answer; his wife was on the *Reinholt,* somewhere in the Sea of Japan. The two Koreans returned to the hospital, took the body to a small graveyard near the outskirts of the city, and buried it.

The 5,000 Korean employees of AMIK also stayed behind. As the Americans left, some Koreans pleaded to be taken, others were silent. They knew that if the North Koreans came those who had worked with the Americans would be in trouble. As it turned out, they were right: Many were never seen again.

Retreating ROK troops straggled through Seoul. The boom of artillery shelling drew near; callers from Washington and Tokyo heard these echoes of war faintly across the telephone lines.

Syngman Rhee left the city and went south. But first he called his ambassador in Washington, Dr. John Myun Chang, and told him to plead with Truman for more aid. It was midafternoon Monday in Washington.

Chang went to see Truman and Acheson. As he told them of his dying countrymen and his collapsing government, he began to weep. The problem, he said, was that his people lacked planes, tanks, and artillery. The aid America had guaranteed months ago had not yet arrived, nor had the munitions Truman and MacArthur had promised the day before.

Truman lectured him patronizingly about the importance of stalwart leadership. He said the war was only two days old and supplies were on their way. Buck up, he said. He pointed out that others "had defended their liberties under much more discouraging situations through to ultimate victory." To illustrate, he referred to the American colonists at Valley Forge in 1777–1778 and the Western Allies in the dark days of 1917. In each case, he noted, things had gotten better shortly afterward. (His two examples may have revealed Truman's inclinations: In both cases foreign aid *and troops,* coming at the crucial moment, helped turn the tide. Perhaps his examples indicated he had already unconsciously concluded he would increase support for Korea. His young aide George Elsey observed him that evening and decided the president was ready to step up assistance. After talking to Truman, Elsey wrote himself a note about the conversation. "The President," he said, "appeared sincerely determined to go very much farther than the initial orders that he had approved for General MacArthur the evening before.")

"This looks very dark and disappointing," Truman told Dr. Chang, "but don't be discouraged, because the United Nations [will] do something. So let's work it out that way." When the Korean ambassador appeared outside moments later, the *New York Times* reporter observed that he looked more cheerful than when he went in.[14]

All day Dean Acheson and his advisers grappled with the crumbling Korean situation and its international implications. Would the Soviet Union enter the war? Was it a Russian feint? How about Formosa? The Philippines? Indochina?

After he left Truman, Acheson returned to his office. He sat by himself for two hours, formulating plans, jotting down notes. At six-thirty he called his advisers in and read them the draft of his recommendations. They agreed with Acheson, something had to be done immediately. Every message from Seoul grew worse. The Republic of Korea was collapsing.[15]

At 7:29 Harry Truman was eating alone at Blair House. The secretary of state called and explained the situation. They agreed the Blair House advisory group should meet again immediately. "Have them here at nine P.M.," Truman said.[16]

Jessup's minutes of the second Blair House session, almost verbatim, provide fascinating insights into the mind of the Truman administration.[17]

As the meeting opened, General Hoyt Vandenberg of the air force proudly reported an American pilot had moments before shot down a North Korean Yak.

"I hope it's not the last," Truman sniffed.

Vandenberg apologized that the young pilots in Korea had not expanded on their implicit orders more aggressively. It was the opening Acheson needed; he began to read his recommendations.

First, he suggested that Truman order the air force and navy to mount a full-scale attack on *all* North Korean forces below the Parallel.

Truman said he agreed.

Vandenberg asked the president whether planes might fly over the Parallel.

No, Truman said, "not yet." (Exactly what he meant by those last two words is unclear, but certainly he was leaving his options open.)

Second, Acheson continued, the Seventh Fleet should sail between Formosa and China, as they had discussed the night before.

Truman agreed. He then mused: Should Formosa be rejoined to Japan? (She had been part of Japan's empire for several generations before 1945.) If so, Formosa would be under MacArthur's command and thus could be protected from an attack by Mao Tse-tung. Chiang Kai-shek would lose his independent position by this move to be sure, but, as Truman admitted, Chiang had recently written him a private letter promising to step down if that would help.

Acheson diplomatically suggested that Truman's idea was

a possibility but that it needed further study. He added he thought it "undesirable" for the United States to become involved in the administration of Formosa.

Truman insisted he was not going to give Chiang a single nickel more. "All the money we [have] given them," he said, "is now invested in United States real estate."

"Or in banks in the Philippine Islands," Louis Johnson chuckled.

Third, Acheson proposed that the United States increase her military forces in the Philippines, and accelerate military aid there. Truman agreed. (So much for the Huk rebels.)

Fourth, the secretary of state continued, the United States should give more aid to Indochina. (Theoretically, so much for Ho Chi Minh.)

Finally, Acheson reported on preparations for tomorrow's UN Security Council meeting. The State Department had drafted a resolution recommending that the UN help South Korea, and Acheson believed it would receive unanimous support. Dean Rusk interjected a comment: If the Russians decided to come to the session to veto the American resolution, the United States could still cover its actions in Korea with the loose wording of the UN Charter.

Truman harrumphed that he rather hoped the Russians *would* veto it. (Beyond a certain childish belligerence, Truman's logic here is unclear.)

The men talked for a while about other possible places the Russians might move against; they also discussed next morning's White House meeting with congressional leaders.

(Throughout this second Blair House conference the civilians from the State Department were the ones pressing for military action. Secretary of Defense Johnson was not even consulted in advance. At the meeting he merely declared that the tone of Acheson's recommendations "suits me," and asked the generals and the admirals in the room what they thought. They had no objections, they replied.

"I don't want to go to war," Truman said. For the last five years, he said, he had done everything he could to avoid just these sorts of decisions. And he repeated that the United States should help South Korea for the sake of the United Nations. (Perhaps by such righteous statements he half convinced himself.)

Truman asked whether he should mobilize the National Guard. He personally was inclined to do so, since he recognized that the United States could not send ground troops to Korea unless it had them available. Bradley quietly suggested it would be better to wait a few days. Truman reluctantly agreed, but told Bradley to consider it.

This second conference has an entirely different tone than the first. The words are harder and a note of satisfaction permeates them. These men had felt frustration for years, had been through a period of forced self-control. Now they displayed primal delight, a kind of orgasmic relief. They were taking Action. A feeling of almost erotic afterglow quietly pulsates through the last few pages of the minutes once the decision had been made to enter the war. There is no evidence that the leaders felt real anxiety. Their anger at Russia now had taken a specific direction. While they were not actually attacking the Soviet Union, this was the next best thing.

They still, however, had not yet committed ground troops.

Douglas MacArthur felt depressed. His confidence and optimism were gone. He even talked of writing off Korea. "All Korea is lost," he told Dulles. "The only thing we can do is get our people safely out of the country." He did not know it, but the picture was about to change. While he saw Dulles off at the airport, a message came from his headquarters to return there for a "teleconference" with Washington. [18]

A teleconference (or telecon) allowed large groups, far

apart, to confer with each other. The telecon's center was an eighteen-by-eighteen-foot room on the Pentagon's third floor. In it was a teletype machine, hooked up to military bases all over the world. A signal corps officer was in charge of the machine. He stood by it, transmitting whatever message had to go out. Replies came back and instantly flashed on a large screen in "clear" (plain English rather than code). Messages stayed on the screen indefinitely, offering the men time to consider their replies carefully, often discussing them at length among themselves. Each response in turn was reproduced on a screen at the other end, in this case Tokyo. Thus a teleconference often lasted several hours, as each side weighed its alternatives and even checked higher authority for approval of this or that point.

Monday night, 10:17. The second Blair House conference had been over almost half an hour. The leaders of America's armed services were in the telecon room; MacArthur and his staff were at the other end. "It was the first time I had ever in person been summoned to such a conference," MacArthur said later, somewhat petulantly.[19]

The men at the Pentagon told MacArthur about the Seventh Fleet and Formosa—and about Korea. "All restrictions which have previously prevented the full utilization of the U.S. Far East Air Forces... are lifted for operations below the 38th Parallel.... The purpose is to clear South Korea of North Korean military forces."[20]

Tokyo radioed KMAG headquarters in Korea: "Momentous decisions are in the offing. Be of good cheer."[21]

As soon as the Blair House conference broke up, Truman phoned his aides and told them to summon certain congressional leaders for a conference the next morning. The following day at precisely eleven-thirty Truman walked into the Cabinet Room, where fourteen senators and congressmen awaited him. Truman had chosen them carefully. Most were members of one of the armed services or foreign relations committees. Eleven military and State Department officials also stood there. They could give advice if necessary, and most of all would provide a display of unity and support.[22]

Truman, uncharacteristically, dispensed with banter. He walked slowly and solemnly around the room, shaking hands and exchanging a few words with each of the politicians. They then sat down around the table, Acheson and Truman side by side at the front.

Truman said he had an important statement to read, but first he asked the secretary of state to summarize the events of the last few days. When Acheson finished, the president scolded him, "But, Dean, you didn't even mention the U.N.!" (The minutes note that Acheson "was quite obviously embarrassed.") Harry Truman the politician recognized something Acheson had overlooked: Truman had not asked the Senate for its advice and consent. Unless he offered some explanation or cover, sensitive senatorial egos might give him trouble in the future. He knew the State Department had a handy list of a hundred precedents for his action, going back to Jefferson, and if pressed he could always fall back on them. (During the following week certain key senators received this list; they used it during congressional debates.) Truman knew, however, it was more prudent to drape his decisions in the UN flag.

After he made his announcements to the congressmen, Truman thanked them and left to go to Blair House for lunch. He awaited reactions.

A question arose later in the week. Did this "support for the UN" involve the United States in a "war"? If so, Truman should have gone to Congress and asked for an official declaration of war. At one point Truman had actually considered asking for some type of congressional resolution. He discussed the possibility with Acheson but the secretary of state talked him out of it. Acheson recalled: "I thought about it, not very deeply, but just enough to come to the conclusion that this was one of those steps like the one more question in cross-examination which destroys you, as a lawyer. . . . Everything was in good shape. . . . The hazards of that step seemed to me far greater than any possible good that could come from it."[23]

Acheson's reasoning provides a classic example of the mentality of the Imperial Presidency. The wise and far-sighted presidential Gulliver had made his decision. It was foolish to ask congressional Lilliputians what they thought about it. Their tiny squeaking could at best only delay things. Besides, they were so tiresome with their questions, their whining, their blatant political posturing, their niggling criticisms, their McCarthyism. Best to ignore them.

Senator William F. Knowland, a conservative and a powerful Republican from California, handed Truman an apparently perfect argument. Knowland was on the floor of the Senate and was temporarily caught up in a burst of enthusiasm for Truman's actions. He said he saw no reason for a congressional declaration of war. The only criticism he had was that the president had limited military activity to the region below the Parallel. As far as he was concerned, Truman should allow the air force to cross the border, just as policemen might chase a burglar away from the scene of a crime. "The action this government is taking," Knowland said, "is a police action against a violator of the law of nations and the Charter of the United Nations." It was a good phrase: police action.[24]

At a press conference that week Truman called the North Koreans "a bunch of bandits." A reporter asked a question: "Mr. President, would it be correct, against your explanation, to call this a police action under the United Nations?"

"Yes, that is exactly what it amounts to."[25]

During the week only a few senators voiced any criticism. Robert Taft, frontrunner for the next Republican presidential nomination, stated only that Truman's decisions reversed Acheson's policies, and therefore the secretary of state should resign. Furthermore, Taft said, Truman should have consulted Congress. Senator McCarthy, Senator William Jenner of Indiana, and a number of spectators in the galleries applauded this speech, but it was an amazingly mild statement.[26]

Almost the only senator to speak violently against Truman on his decision was Senator Jenner. For a long time Jenner had sustained a reputation for his angry denunciations of Commies and pinkos. His political stance lay somewhat to the right of Cardinal Richelieu, and his speeches were nasty and often inaccurate. Each morning he apparently gargled with hogwash. (Lately, he had been even more vitriolic. He might have become concerned that McCarthy was getting so many headlines. Jenner had been Red-baiting for years when the junior senator from Wisconsin discovered the issue. Suddenly Jenner was a political cuckold: Joe McCarthy had run off with his true love.) On Friday of that week Jenner addressed the Indiana Republican convention. The senator demanded Acheson's ouster and the removal of his crowd of "Fair Deal fanatics who want to remake America from within and the miserable scheming, conniving, state department personnel who have helped to force the crisis upon us."[27]

Most reactions to Truman's announcement were positive. Democrats were particularly enthusiastic. Senator Lyndon Johnson wrote the president: "I want to express to you my deep gratitude for and admiration of your courageous response yesterday to the challenge of this grave hour." He added, "Having chosen this course, there is no turning back."[28]

Hubert Humphrey was almost transfixed by Truman's announcement. "I believe this is a fatal hour," he said. "I pray God in all reverence that all the people will give their support to this policy." He concluded thunderously, "This may be the greatest move for peace in the twentieth century."[29]

Republicans were also pleased. Styles Bridges, senator

from New Hampshire and a constant critic of the administration, was at the Tuesday conference in the Cabinet Room. As he left he told reporters, "I think it is a damned good action."[30]

Arthur Vandenberg lay dying. As Republican leader of the Senate Foreign Relations Committee, for years he had been his party's chief spokesman on foreign affairs. On July 3 he wrote Truman a personal letter praising the decision as a "courageous and indispensable thing."[31]

On Wake Island John Foster Dulles received the news at breakfast. A companion later described his reaction. "Mr. Dulles completely forgot that he was a Republican. At that moment, in his mind, President Truman was the greatest president in history."[32]

Congress in general was elated and acted accordingly. When Truman's statement was read to the members of the House, they literally stood up and cheered. Within a day both houses overwhelmingly passed a selective service act that had been deadlocked for weeks.

Joseph Harsch, a reporter for the *Christian Science Monitor,* described what happened in the capital that week:

> I have lived and worked in and out of this city for 20 years. Never before in that time have I felt such a sense of relief and unity pass through this city. . . .
> I have never seen such a large part of Washington so nearly satisfied with a decision of the government.[33]

Outside the government, reactions were about the same. When Truman addressed the annual meeting of the Reserve Officers Association, the organization's leader asked the assembled officers whether they supported the president, and they leaped to their feet in a shouting, standing ovation. Truman received more than 1,200 letters and telegrams, overwhelmingly favorable.[34] The amount of response, considering the seriousness of the issue, was hardly staggering, but the percentage of approval was pleasant.

(Yet there was also a strange apathy. After the House's initial applause, its members sat back and hardly even discussed the matter for the rest of the week. Apparently they considered it momentarily exciting but essentially inconsequential—like making love with your spouse.)

Leaders in Western Europe, when they first heard of the civil war in Korea, had apparently been concerned that the United States would *not* act. Acheson claimed that they "appeared to be in a state of near-panic."[35] When Truman announced that he had entered the war, the British House of Commons cheered. And when Prime Minister Clement Attlee told it the next day that his cabinet had "decided to support the United States" (note: not the UN) with the navy, again cheers erupted; even Winston Churchill rose slowly to his feet and sonorously growled his support.[36]

In Paris, when Ambassador David Bruce told Robert Schuman, the French foreign minister burst into tears. "Thank God," he said, "this will not be a repetition of the past."[37]

Averell Harriman, in Paris at the time, could not stand the thought of missing all the excitement in Washington. He called Acheson and pleaded with him, saying he just had to get back immediately. The secretary of state granted his request. Within twelve hours he was in the United States.[38]

Early in the day a crowd began to gather outside the UN. Ushers squeezed 1,200 spectators into seats inside; they turned away 5,000.

Several miles away, at a restaurant called the Stockholm, two dozen diplomats were eating an uneasy lunch. Weeks before, Konstantin Zinchenko, the assistant secretary general for Security Council affairs, a Russian, had arranged a nonpolitical luncheon. He had invited nine of the eleven Security Council delegates. (He ignored the Chinese and Yugoslav delegations, neither of which the Soviet Union recognized.) He also invited some Secretariat associates like Trygve Lie and some high-ranking Soviet officials including Yakov Malik, the dour Russian delegate. Officially, the Soviet Union had not attended UN meetings since January, when Malik stalked out in an apparent fury that the UN refused to seat the representative for Mao's China. Unofficially, of course, the Russians remained in New York and followed events closely.

One of the main fears at the State Department during this week was that Malik would chose this moment to return and exercise his right to veto Security Council decisions. Last Sunday, State officials had worried that Malik might suddenly come and veto the initial resolution on Korea. They had decided that if he came, they would turn to the General Assembly for a decision; it would be chancier and should be avoided if possible, but they would do it if necessary. When Sunday's resolution had passed without any problem they had been relieved. If Malik showed up now and stopped today's motion, they would merely fall back on Sunday's vote, but they were still anxious, for it would not have quite the same public-relations impact.

Their anxiety made the Stockholm lunch quite tense. Trygve Lie, obviously trying to smooth over past differences, kept urging Malik to attend. Ernest Gross glared at Lie and tried to signal him to cease. He did everything but wiggle his eyebrows. As it was, Malik did not go to the UN that day.

The usual, if somewhat dubious, explanation for this Soviet failure to veto either of the week's resolutions has been that the clunking Russian bureaucracy moved too slowly. Such an explanation, if true, would indicate that the Kremlin was unprepared for (and perhaps surprised by) North Korea's attack. This possibility in turn weakens the administration's claim that it became involved in Korea to stop Soviet expansionism. (But even assuming that the Russians were surprised by the attack, Malik's strange absence on Tuesday—four days after the war began—is curious.)

The Security Council session opened shortly after three. Warren Austin, United States ambassador to the UN, presented Washington's motion. The statement recommended that "Members of the United Nations furnish such assistance to the Republic of Korea as may be necessary to repel the armed attack and to restore international peace and security in the area."

The session lasted all day and into the night. Two delegations waited for instructions from their governments: India and Egypt. The representative from Yugoslavia opposed the American resolution as premature. He introduced a resolution suggesting mediation. By 11:45, under American pressure, the Security Council voted; it was 7 to 1 with 2 abstentions. The Egyptian and Indian representatives, still without their government's orders, merely passed.

By the time the delegates tiredly voted, American planes were already flying missions over Korea.

CHAPTER EIGHT

Through the Looking Glass

KEYES BEECH: I hate to say this, Burton, but this is the first time I've felt alive since Iwo.
BURTON CRANE: I know what you mean.

—Keyes Beech, *Tokyo and Points East*
(1954)

SEOUL WAS an anthill, scattered by war.

Rumors skittered around: The North Koreans were already at the gates. (As a matter of fact they would not arrive for almost twenty-four hours, but few could know for certain.) Darkness added to the dread. Refugees clogged the streets leading out of town. Looters scrambled through the city, snatching valuables, almost anything portable. (Korea was a poor country in the best of times; war made it worse. Cans of food, tires, a chair, a forgotten toothbrush—each item had its use to a hungry and terrified citizenry.) The chaos in the city worsened when government leaders fled.

Early Tuesday morning, in the stillness before dawn, Syngman Rhee left Seoul by train without consulting his government or telling Ambassador Muccio. When his cabinet heard the news, they met to discuss whether they should leave too. If they withdrew to the South, they could avoid being caught up in the maelstrom of battle. They might remain a viable government. Once they were gone, the army could blow up the bridges across the Han River and fight the enemy in the streets of the city. Buildings and basements make splendid fortresses, and as they turn to rubble they offer more rather than fewer opportunities for snipers and defensive counterattacks. The Russians proved the truth of that during World War II; so did the Germans. A courageous defense of a city could slow an attacker for weeks. Who could know what might happen in the meantime? The North Koreans had stretched their supply lines out along the highways. These could be cut. American aid, especially antitank weapons and planes, could make a difference. Around four in the morning the cabinet decided to leave. Most members of the National Assembly trickled after. The first of two special trains pulled out of Seoul shortly after dawn. [1]

Before they departed, three Korean officials drove to the American embassy. As they arrived they saw the flames of a bonfire burning fiercely in the parking lot. Members of the embassy staff staggered around carrying secret papers and documents and flinging them into the fire. Boxes and suitcases formed jumbled piles in the hallways inside. As Americans scurried back and forth around them, the three Koreans told Muccio that Rhee had already departed and that the cabinet was about to leave. They looked at the scramble around them and said goodbye.

Muccio ordered all but a tiny remnant of his staff to fly out of Kimpo right away. He considered staying in Seoul to the end, allowing himself to be captured if necessary, but Acheson wired him to follow the Korean government wherever it went. He divided his skeleton staff into two groups and sent one south to follow Rhee's government; he himself would come later on.

The ambassador ate lunch and talked briefly to Sterling Wright, chief of KMAG, at his headquarters. As they were speaking two North Korean Yak planes flew past, strafing the buildings. The two men leaped beneath nearby desks. "Mr. Ambassador," Wright said, "I thing we'd better get out of here."[2]

About three-thirty Muccio left the city in his own Mercury. Behind him, the American embassy lay vacant and locked. Iron shutters covered the doors and windows like closed eyelids on a corpse.

During the afternoon General Chae Pyong Dok, "Fat" Chae, ex–*sumo* wrestler and head of the Korean army, tired, confused, and jumpy, decided to withdraw his headquarters from the city. By doing so he cut communications with his men in the field. He still had units fighting north of Seoul. Although they were pulling slowly back ahead of the tanks, most of them retained their weapons and even their fighting spirit. With them, Chae might have held the city, or at least the Han River line just south of it. By pulling back he almost guaranteed the city's fall. His irrational panic did not cause South Korea's defeat, but it greatly contributed to it. Chae was a decent, brave man who genuinely wanted to do what was right—if he only knew what that was. In a few weeks, demoted and dishonored, he would be dead, killed in a skirmish defending a roadblock.

When Sterling Wright, quiet and able, realized Chae was withdrawing, he made two decisions. He ordered most of his KMAG to fly to Japan. He would stay with a handful of men and follow the ROK army.

As Wright drove from the capital searching for Chae's command, he received the "Momentous decisions are in the offing" message from MacArthur implying the United States was about to increase its military involvement. Wright contacted the airport and told KMAG officers there to return immediately to Seoul. An observer at the airfield, watching them climb into their jeeps as the rain came down around them, recalled, "I have never seen a sadder, more dispirited bunch of men than that KMAG group as they started north to Seoul again. They were almost sure that the battle was lost and that they were being ordered to a duty which would bring them death or imprisonment."[3]

Wright found General Chae, and using MacArthur's note persuaded the Korean to return to Seoul and hold out. By six o'clock they were all back in the city. They waited for developments.

At seven-thirty the first probing North Korean unit reached the outskirts of Seoul. It withdrew under heavy fire from ROK forces. About eleven o'clock a North Korean tank along with a platoon of infantry filtered into the northeast corner of the capital near the zoo. A Korean constabulary police unit managed to blow up the tank and scatter the enemy infantry. The battle for Seoul had begun.

During the evening members of the ROK staff became frenzied as reports came in of fierce action along the city's limits. All they could think of was the tanks. They could visualize them clanking right through the city and across the Han bridges. Seoul would then be surrounded. They wanted to destroy the bridges. Especially the main one, the massive Han River Bridge, three lanes leading out of the city and eight lanes of traffic moving into it.

At that moment the bridge and the area around it appeared like a medieval painting of hell. Even in daylight Seoul was a bleak and tired town, designed by the Japanese occupation to be functional. Americans had merely appropriated what was there and added little to it. Here in the blackness, a soft rain falling, the low silhouettes of the city's drab, gray-stone, government buildings hulked in the background, almost ominous in their weathered, flaking shabbiness. They were the seedy whores left behind by two armies, one Japanese, one American. The darkness lay heavy, unbroken by street lamps, only scissored now and then by the headlights of trucks or jeeps crawling past.

Noise filled the night. Units of the South Korean army, by horseback and by vehicle, stretched across the bridge. They jammed all three lanes, fender to fender, moving south. They were orderly; they had not yet become a panic-stricken army in flight. They were merely making a strategic retreat. Their trucks and artillery trailed back behind them into the inky recesses of the city. It would be hours before they would all get across the river.

As the military vehicles inched slowly ahead, thousands of civilians surrounded them, oozing into every crevice of space on the roads and the bridge. These were the Korean refugees, fleeing the sounds of artillery fire, their belongings packed in tight little balls. Withered old women and bawling babies. Frightened children lost in the darkness crying for their mothers, like a herd of cattle in a stockyard pressing toward a ramp, like an audience in a burning theater, streaming toward the narrow exits, eyes glazed, nostrils widened in pulsating terror, this jostle of Korean humanity jammed together, shuffling ahead, away from War, toward Life.

Among them were three American journalists: Burton Crane of the *New York Times,* Frank Gibney of *Life,* and Keyes Beech of the *Chicago Daily News.* They, along with Marguerite Higgins of the *Herald Tribune,* had just flown into Korea about six hours earlier. They had landed at dusk aboard the last plane coming to pick up American evacuees at Kimpo Airport. The first thing they noticed at the desolate airfield was the litter of punctured beer cans and cardboard boxes left behind by departing Americans. When they arrived in Seoul they saw Colonel Wright. This was immediately after Wright had gotten MacArthur's "be of good cheer" message. He told the reporters things were "fluid" at the moment but looked hopeful. The four correspondents thanked him and went off to bed.

About one-thirty in the morning an officer woke the three men, who were at KMAG headquarters—Wright had persuaded Higgins to stay at his home, which had more room—and told them the city was about to fall. "They're in the city," he said. "Head for Suwon." As they raced for the stairs they noticed a tiny sign tacked to a bulletin board: "Don't Forget Tuesday June 27 Bingo." The three dove into a jeep and soon were driving toward the bridge. At 2:15 they were on it.[4]

At the ROK army building several Koreans argued angrily with growing impatience. "Fat" Chae had left again. He had taken a jeep and crossed the river. His deputy, Kim Paik Il, was in charge. Suddenly a division commander walked into the room to find out what was happening. Kim told him the bridges were about to blow—the vice minister of defense, a civilian official connected to the cabinet, had ordered them dynamited. The division commander became frantic. At this moment, he said, his unit, the Second Division, was crossing the Han River Bridge. General Kim *must* countermand the vice minister's orders. They must *not* destroy the bridge until he had gotten his troops and their equipment across the river. At last Kim agreed. He turned and ordered a subordinate to race to the bridge to stop them from detonating the explosives. The junior officer left the building, took a jeep, and entered the milling traffic outside. At 2:15 he was 150 yards from the bridge.[5]

Marguerite Higgins was asleep when Sterling Wright's aide ran in. "Get up!" he exclaimed. "They've broken through—we have to run for it." Higgins and the aide charged toward a jeep.

Wright was asleep for the first time in days. As calls came in for him from KMAG headquarters, no one woke him out of consideration for his exhaustion. When at last they told him about the bridge, he scrambled to his feet and started to drive toward his headquarters. It was 2:15.[6]

The blast opened a vast yellow hole in the night. Flames crackled toward the sky. Out of the rain and darkness, for a moment one could see the bridge rise and twist, could see hundreds of bodies flung in the air, rag dolls spinning into space. Then blackness again.

Sound erupted. Screams of terror, of pain. Korean voices in the rain. The shrieking of death. Blood. Madness. What had been a mighty four-span bridge had become a gnarled wreckage. People had become the same.

One of the injured was Sergeant Leroy Deans of Alice, Texas, twenty-two years old, part of the advisory group. Two weeks later the *New York Times* reported that Sergeant Deans received a Purple Heart for an eye wound he sustained when the bridge blew. Officially he was his country's first wounded soldier.[7]

Burton Crane, one of the journalists on the bridge, described what happened to him: "Our correspondents' jeep, only 25 yards from the blast, was protected by a large truck full of soldiers, all of whom died. The explosion blew the windshield back into my face and that of Mr. Gibney." It rolled the jeep back fifteen feet and wrecked it. "I'm hit," Crane said, "I can't see. There's blood in my eyes." Flying glass had gashed Gibney and Crane around the face and head; blood dripped down on their chests and legs. Keyes Beech, in the back seat, was unscathed. He took an undershirt from his bag for Crane's cut and led him by the hand away from the smoking bridge.[8]

Maggie Higgins was still enveloped in the mob behind the bridge when it blew. "My God," said the young lieutenant with her.[9] What General Kim's assistant, who had gone to the bridge to stop the demolition, said is unrecorded.

It was an immense human tragedy. It was also a military disaster. Almost all the equipment of the ROK army was marooned north of the Han River. Most of the troops eventually got across but they were scattered and increasingly discouraged. Valid estimates of their numbers at this time ran around 40,000, but these were soldiers with little or no artillery and less and less organization. They had fought bravely for days. They had not been overwhelmed. They were not routed, not even yet. But unless they had time to regroup and rearm, they would be ineffective. (If the North Koreans had not lingered to resupply themselves, to organize the capital and repair the bridges, the war might have been over in a matter of several days.)

Who was responsible? General Chae had crossed the main bridge only a few minutes before it went up. He knew it was set for destruction. If he did not personally order it blown up as he drove away, he certainly did not stop it. To be sure, the vice minister of defense, perhaps following directions from the cabinet, may have given the initial orders, but Chae, knowing their devastating military impact, could have countermanded them, just as General Kim attempted to do. Poor "Fat" Chae, exhausted, confused, possibly a trifle frightened. The following day, he personally accepted the blame. (Maybe it is only romantic foolishness to wonder if his death a few weeks later, as he personally defended the retreat of a small South Korean unit, was an attempt to regain his self-esteem.) In September his government, attempting to affix blame for the incident, with Chae already dead, tried, convicted, and executed their army chief engineer.[10]

Sterling Wright gathered his men together, almost sixty of them, and set out in a convoy to find some other way across. They drove for hours back and forth. Eventually they decided to ferry across. At the river's edge near the blackened, misshapen bridge, shoving their way through a terrified mass of screaming, pushing Koreans, they tried to persuade a boatman to take them over. In the darkness, amidst the surging humanity struggling to find any method to escape, it seemed impossible. When a boat, a raft, or even a log turned up at the water's edge, so many people grabbed at it many vessels merely swamped and sank. To help Wright, a Korean Colonel named Lee Chi Up took direct action. He raised his gun and fired at one of the boatmen. The bullet went through the man's shirt; the boatman brought the raft over to them. (Whether this was a lucky hit or a lucky miss is not clear.) Colonel Wright put almost all his men and Maggie Higgins on the raft and told them to leave without him, he was going to try to bring his radio truck. As the Americans started to go, the Koreans on the bank tried to clamber on the raft and were only held back at gunpoint. (Wright got across a little later on another raft.)[11]

All day Wednesday Americans from Seoul staggered into Suwon, a town about twenty miles south of the capital. There they met General John Church. MacArthur originally had picked Church to lead a survey team to Korea to report on the war. When Truman had expanded his orders, MacArthur delegated Church to take control of all American forces in Korea.

Church was not particularly prepossessing. He was thin and stooped. His hair receded from his somewhat sloping forehead; his high cheekbones accentuated his narrow, homely face—he looked more like a Tennessee mountain farmer than a major general. Nor was he unduly bright or imaginative. He was MacArthur's direct source of information, and his perceptions of the war had great impact.

Throughout the day Church talked to KMAG officers as they arrived. He learned of the destruction of the bridges; he saw Korean soldiers straggle by; he met poor, tired General Chae. He concluded solely from this evidence—possibly correctly, perhaps not—that the South Korean cause was lost. He radioed MacArthur that the only way to win the war was to send American GIs. Tokyo sent him back a message: MacArthur himself would arrive in Suwon the next morning. [12]

Thursday morning. Tokyo.

Douglas MacArthur got up while it was still dark and drove to the airport. He was excited, the adrenalin was pumping through his aging body. He was off to war. A careful and perceptive observer described how he looked that day: "MacArthur seemed buoyant. His eyes possessed that same luminous brilliance which I had sometimes seen in the faces of fever patients."[13] His plane left at 6:10. Several other generals and four favored reporters accompanied him. Somewhere around 4,000 feet he took out his bag, reached in, and withdrew his old corncob pipe.[14] Along with his crushed hat, which he was now wearing, the pipe had become a famous symbol during the last war, his trademark. The fact that he took it with him to Korea is interesting. He remembers that as he sat back and lit it someone exclaimed, "Haven't seen you smoke that pipe, General, for years!"

"I don't dare smoke it back there in Tokyo," he said. "They'd think I was nothing but a farmer."[15]

It was a sly, disingenuous reply. The old general obviously had that corncob pipe out in public for many reasons. He might have gotten some reassurance from its familiar feel and maybe gained a sense of strength from it. The pipe was associated with the golden days of the war in the Pacific. It hinted of vigor and victory. It probably gave him a certain amount of security. He certainly knew it would have that effect on others. It also had other uses. In conversations he pointed its long thin stem at others like a stiletto. The effect was decisive, impressive, and slightly intimidating. MacArthur was a crafty practitioner of image molding. Almost everyone who saw him that day later remarked on that simple, homey corncob. (American advertising had lost a genius when MacArthur applied to West Point.)

While his plane, *Bataan*, was in the air, MacArthur talked to George Stratemeyer, head of the air force in the Far East. MacArthur listened as Stratemeyer complained that his pilots were not having great success. Weather and distance accounted for part of the problem, but the main difficulty, he said, was that such important and vulnerable targets as supply depots and air bases were across the Parallel in North Korea. His orders had been to stay below the line, but these directions were too restrictive and kept him from succeeding. MacArthur agreed. He unhesitatingly dictated a cablegram that Stratemeyer wrote down and handed to the *Bataan's* pilot for immediate transmission: "Stratemeyer to [Major General Earl E.] Partridge: Take out North Korean Airfield immediately. No publicity. MacArthur approves."[16]

MacArthur thus went beyond his orders. In theory this decision was only a military one, involving a rather simple tactical matter. In fact it contained major strategic connotations which altered the meaning of the war. Pilots had first been directed only to protect the evacuation; then they had been told to *search out* enemy planes and tanks. The first task had been to help Americans, the second to aid Korean troops in the field. Now MacArthur was sending planes to destroy the war-making capabilities of North Korea. He had, moreover, bypassed the White House. Truman's later problems with his general, leading to MacArthur's removal, can be seen here.

Four hours or so after the *Bataan* left Tokyo, it settled down at the Suwon airport. Waiting there were General Church, John Muccio, and Syngman Rhee. (The American ambassador and the Korean president had just arrived themselves.) The entire group met at Church's headquarters in a nearby building, where chairs had been arranged in rows and maps were tacked up on the walls. The briefing began. Church and several of his officers described various specific military matters—transportation, supply, intelligence. Rhee spoke. Even General Chae spoke, though few Americans listened to him. (A loser, particularly a drooping fat one like the Korean general, repels Americans, who tend to believe that losing not only leaves an almost ineradicable taint of humiliation but is also contagious.) "We ought to get rid of that fellow," MacArthur said. Even as Chae talked, although he did not know it, his replacement was on his way.[17]

After hearing reports for more than an hour MacArthur became impatient. "Let's go to the front and have a look," he said.[18] He got into the back of an old Ford sedan and drove north, followed by a string of jeeps filled with middle-aged generals, tired foreign service officers, and excited correspondents and photographers. The convoy must have looked imposing to Koreans who trooped past heading the other way. As the Americans sped by, their faces set, grim, and determined, Korean civilians and soldiers alike sometimes stopped and cheered. The Yanks had landed. The generals were here. If brass alone—or reporters—could win this war the soldiers from the Democratic People's Republic might as well lay down their arms.

When MacArthur's band reached a spot several hundred yards from the Han River it stopped. MacArthur stood atop a hill and gazed across the river at Seoul. Smoke from the city drifted toward the sky, the distant cough of mortars carried over the water. Rafts of every description still converged on the south bank far below beneath his feet. Lines of soldiers and civilians clambered slowly past him and meandered down the road to Suwon. A colonel offered MacArthur his binoculars, but the proud general snapped, "I see perfectly."[19] Photographers stood below him on the hill snapping his picture. His pose, staring out toward Seoul, thoughtful, serious, almost regal in his contemplation, was like some statue's. (What does it do to a man to become a monument during his own lifetime?)

After a while he turned and walked back to his car. He

had seen—and been seen—enough. He was ready to return to Tokyo. As the *Bataan* flew toward Japan, MacArthur began to compose a message for Washington. (The note did not go out until the next morning. Why he waited quite so long is unclear. It was late when he arrived in Tokyo, so possibly he went to bed while his aides finished drafting it. More likely he decided to wait overnight before sending his gloomy analysis. The South Koreans might miraculously counterattack and make it unnecessary to send it.)

In Washington Louis Johnson heard about the fall of Seoul. He suggested another meeting to Truman. After forty-five minutes with the National Security Council, Truman gave his approval to two significant new directives. [20]

First, air and naval units were now allowed to make attacks north of the Parallel. Truman knew MacArthur's planes were already bombing Pyongyang. He probably decided merely to accept Tokyo's actions rather than fight them.

Second, he ordered small combat units to guard the port facilities and airfield at Pusan on the southern tip of Korea, to guarantee the safety of those Americans still evacuating from there and to protect the supply line to Korea.

At 10:50 that night the message from MacArthur arrived in Washington. It was long and rambling but it said in part:

> The South Korean forces are in confusion, have not seriously fought and lack leadership. . . .
> The Korean Army is entirely incapable of counter-action and there is a grave danger of a further breakthrough.
> The only assurance for holding the present line . . . is through the introduction of US Ground Combat Forces into the Korean battle area. [21]

General Collins, army chief of staff, read the note and recognized its significance. MacArthur was requesting a full-blown fighting war. He wanted more than planes or ships, more than a handful of advisers or tiny defensive units—he wanted infantrymen with rifles.

Although the time was almost midnight Collins arranged a teleconference. It began at 3:40 A.M. In Tokyo MacArthur sat with six members of his staff. At the Pentagon were Collins, Dean Rusk, and several others. Those who waited in the darkened telecon room in Washington realized the historic nature of the moment. Collins remembers that there was "an eerie quality" in the air. The men in the room "instinctively spoke with hushed voices as the questions, numbered serially, were flashed on the screen."[22]

Collins told Tokyo that MacArthur's request would require presidential approval, and Truman would want to consult his advisers before he gave it. (Collins was obviously not anxious to wake a dozen superiors unless absolutely necessary.) Couldn't MacArthur merely start the process of sending troops to Pusan, using his present authorization? Collins would have the president's reply before troops actually left Japan. MacArthur haughtily indicated that such an arrangement would not be satisfactory; he wanted a decision "without delay."

While the others in the telecon room waited, intently watching the screen, Collins left and phoned Omar Bradley, chairman of the Joint Chiefs. (The famous "Buck" began to be passed.) Bradley agreed that the matter was important enough to phone Secretary of the Army Pace. (The Buck was moving ever higher.) At 4:57 Pace called Truman and woke him up. (The Buck came to rest.)

"Mr. President, I'm sorry to get you up at this hour," Pace apologized.

Truman brushed his concern aside with "It's my responsibility to be ready in an emergency."[23]

Pace explained MacArthur's request to use battle troops in Korea. Harry Truman, probably the champion decision maker ever to live in the White House, a man who could insist he dropped the atom bomb on Hiroshima "like that" and snap his fingers, did not hesitate. He instantly authorized MacArthur to send a regimental combat team to the front. As for the two divisions Tokyo referred to, he would send a reply in a few hours. Pace called Collins back; the army chief of staff returned to the murky telecon room and informed MacArthur of Truman's decision.[24]

"Acknowledged," Tokyo replied.

Friday, 9:30 A.M.

Truman met with his top advisers; the conference only lasted half an hour. (This group, with a few exceptions like Harriman, who was now attending, had gathered almost every day since Sunday. Each meeting was shorter than the one before.) It seemed more as if they were ironing out details than giving full consideration to broader implications. As the week progressed they still talked about the Russians, the Chinese, and the situation in Iran, but their debates smacked a little of formal, bureaucratic sessions. They appeared to be going through the motions. Psychologically they probably could not turn back. Their emotions, to say nothing of their reputations, were on the line. If MacArthur, the general on the scene, determined that he needed two divisions—or four—or eight—so be it. Truman approved MacArthur's request.[25]

Early in the war *Life* magazine sent reporters out to feel the pulse of Americana. As their "representative" community, they chose Sycamore, Illinois, a town laid out in nice neat squares on the flat plains fifty miles west of Chicago, population about 6,000, almost totally white, Anglo-Saxon, and Protestant. Sycamore was dominated by neither farmers nor industrialists; it was neither poor nor prosperous. It was just a classic, average Midwestern town. (One can almost hear the palms at Time-Life, Inc., rubbing in satisfaction.) The populace of Sycamore, or at least those who were asked, almost unanimously supported Truman's actions in Korea. They saw the war as a matter of opposing Russian expansionism. One man, a fifty-eight-year-old tailor named George W. Roden, put the thinking of Sycamore, Illinois (and perhaps the United States), into words. "Sure I got boys, and son-in-law, too," he said. "I still agree with Truman. We have let Russia get too many countries, and too many footholds. We ought to protect those countries and get those commies out of there. We ought to let those people in Europe and Asia own their own countries, but we ought to see they get good rulers. And when they have an election we ought to see that they have a fair and honest election. That's what this country's for."[26] Few philosophers have ever put it more eloquently—all the things that were best and worst in America: the idealism, the incredible pride, the faith in political decisions, in "good rulers," in "a fair and honest election," and most of all, in America's right and even obligation to guarantee these things. To men like George W. Roden, who was clearly not at all enthusiastic about this war, the American Way had become a religion—with icons and priestlike politicians muttering cabalistic phrases ("liberty," "free enterprise," "public opinion," "Coca-Cola"). To disseminate this Way was to engage in a grim Holy War. It was not a Splendid Little War, nor a Great Crusade: It was only—somehow—"necessary."

PART TWO: TO BATTLE

CHAPTER NINE

An
Arrogant
Display

I threw in troops from the Twenty-fourth Division by air in the hope of
establishing a locus of resistance around which I could rally the fast-
retreating South Korean forces.

I also hoped by that arrogant display of strength to fool the enemy into
belief that I had a much greater resource at my disposal than I did.

—Douglas MacArthur

THE HEAVY AIR WAS sultry in Japan. At Camp Wood on
Kyushu Island Brad Smith's wife shook him awake. "Colonel Stephens is on the phone and wants you," she whispered. When Smith groggily answered the phone, his commanding officer told him, "The lid has blown off." He was
to take half a battalion to Itazuke air base not far away,
where General William Dean, head of the entire division,
would give him further orders. [1]

Smith told his wife, then got ready to go. At age thirty-
four, he was about to enter his second war.

When Brad Smith was twelve, he made a decision: When
he grew up, he wanted to go to West Point. From that

moment on he badgered local politicians in his Lambertville, New Jersey, region, asking for their support. But when he graduated from high school in 1932, West Point did not take him.

Lambertville is a Delaware River town, twelve miles north of Trenton, situated amid the green flatlands in the western part of the state. An unassuming town at best, in the depression year of 1932 Lambertville did not offer much to this rather thin sixteen-year-old high school graduate. Young Brad took a clerk's job in Wollaston's Drug Store on the corner of Main and Church streets, flirted with some of the local girls, helped ladies with their packages, shelved laxatives in nice straight rows, and sold traveling salesmen Trojan prophylactics, three for a quarter. He was unsatisfied. For the next three years he wrote letters, filled out forms, and pestered congressmen, and finally in 1935 he was accepted at West Point.

Smith—or "Smitty," as they called him at the Academy—was normally friendly and pleasant. He wore his light brown curly hair in a high mop, the kind that was popular among boys from Lambertville. His face was long and rectangular, dominated by a large forehead, thick eyebrows, and a prominent curved nose. He was not very bright. He worked hard but still graduated from West Point 384th out of 456. He opted for the infantry, the usual home of the lower quarter of each class.

On December 7, 1941, he was stationed at Schofield Barracks, a mile or so from the naval base of Pearl Harbor. When the Japanese attack came, he helped form troops into defensive positions on a spot known as Barber's Point, in case of an amphibious or parachute assault.

Later on he married Bettie Evans of Pasadena, California. By 1950 they had two sons, Craig (just school age) and Brian (barely perambulatory, still in that lurching stage of the toddler).[2] The four of them had just arrived at Camp Wood.

In Kumamoto Lieutenant Phil Day's pregnant wife finished fixing supper and the two sat down to eat. The phone rang. Day was to return immediately to camp, he was being ordered to Korea. The dinner lay ruined on the table.

Phil Day was twenty-four years old, only two years out of West Point and untested in battle.[3]

Segments of the Twenty-first Regiment gathered at Camp Wood. It was a Friday night. They had all been paid a few hours earlier and most had received passes. They were in town drinking or with their "mooses" when their orders came through. They sped back to base and scurried through their barracks packing their equipment. Many were drunk, a few were sick. In the time-honored tradition of soldiers everywhere, they swore at the situation and the army and each other, and they climbed into waiting trucks, to sit huddled in the dark, shoulders hunched down, tense. Scuttlebutt had been right; they were going to Korea, going to drop right in there, kick some gooks, and get out. It shouldn't take long; this was the U.S. Army. They'd be back in a week or two. They'd better be—otherwise, what would happen to their mooses, their sweet little Jap gals?

It won't take long. Just about everybody thought so. Some of the men took only two clips of ammunition. They did not want to weigh themselves down with extraneous material. They had no real fear of the North Koreans. One participant later said, "We thought they'd back off as soon as they saw American uniforms."[4] Another later admitted, "I regarded the episode as an adventure that would probably last only a few days."[5] It would be a snap.

The Twenty-first Regiment belonged to an army which—they were told—had won every war it entered. This army, which had beaten the pride of the Nazis, now only faced North Koreans. The men at Camp Wood, waiting in their trucks, were confident.

The winds rose, the sky became blacker, and the patter of

rain became a roar. The monsoons had arrived. About three in the morning the trucks began to roll. Behind them they left the unhappiness and confusion of altered lives. The mooses in Kumamoto suddenly found themselves without any money for food or rent. Those with babies were in despair.

(Some American wives fell apart. All those living in town were sent to Camp Wood with their children and placed in empty bachelor-officer quarters. Here, amidst overcrowding and dirty diapers, children who missed their fathers became hysterical, women began to drink. In the tensions of uncertainty they fought among themselves, and waited for word from Korea.[6])

General Dean was at Itazuke when the trucks pulled in. He told Smith the task force was to fly to the city of Pusan on the southern tip of Korea. Dean did not know exactly where the enemy was, but he ordered Smith to move "as far north as possible" to come to grips with them. He was to slow or stop the North Korean advance. "Sorry I can't give you more information," Dean said. "That's all I've got. Good luck to you, and God bless you and your men."[7]

At the airfield planes were revving their engines. The men of Task Force Smith clambered down from their trucks, hitched their shoulder straps into less uncomfortable positions, and took off for Korea.

Pusan took on a holiday atmosphere as they arrived. Posters and banners fluttered everywhere. Cheap American flags flapped from windows and sprouted from the fists of cheering people massed along the roadways. At the railroad station Korean bands blared and whistled and drummed their pleasure at the presence of Americans—these terribly young, relatively untrained and unprepared troops of the Twenty-first Regiment. The Americans were convinced they were about to win a great victory, and so were the enthusiastic Koreans.

About eight that evening their train pulled out of the station, chugging and hissing its way north for twelve hours while most of the soldiers slept where they sat. A few inevitable poker games began and some GIs joked back and forth in the way of young American males far from home. The windows of the train, blackened by a cloudy, starless night, reflected their faces. With the Korean landscape invisible, they might have been on their way from Fort Dix to some army post in the Southwest, perhaps Oklahoma or Texas. Inside a train rushing through the night all countries look about the same; the contours of Korea could have been Kentucky or New York or Oregon.

Next morning the train screeched its brakes and pulled into the Japanese-made gray-stone railway station at Taejon. This city was the temporary capital of South Korea. Its population in 1949 had been 126,704, but now it was swollen with refugees pouring in from the North. The morning was rainy but the reception at Taejon was even wilder than the Pusan sendoff. The troops were welcomed by several United Nations officials as well as by Sihn Sung, Korea's acting premier. Again crowds were on hand to cheer, again a Korean brass band played what it understood to be stirring American favorites: "Dixie" and "Columbia, the Gem of the Ocean."

A lieutenant colonel directed Brad Smith to American military headquarters in Taejon, one room in a two-story, yellow brick building also housing the South Korean government. Smith met General John Church, still in charge of American efforts in Korea. The general seemed confident. He told reporters a few hours later, "We will hurl back the North Koreans, and if the Russkies intervene we will hurl them back too."[8]

When Smith arrived, Church was conferring with several American and South Korean officers about the military situation. The outlook seemed grim. ROK troops were not only falling back, but in some sectors were in headlong, panicky retreat. Church, always a taciturn man, greeted Smith briefly, turned to a map, pointed north along the main highway near Seoul, and said, "We have a little action up here. All we need is some men up there who won't run when they see tanks." (He obviously was referring to the South Korean retreat. He could not hide his disdain for Koreans.) "We're going to move you up to support the ROKs and give them moral support."[9] This was the extent of Smith's orders. They reflected one of the major misconceptions which American leaders—from Harry Truman on down—had about the war. Americans assumed it was merely going to be a matter of an appearance on the battlefield, where a relative handful of them would break the thrust of North Korea's attack. Even General MacArthur used the same kind of language. As he later told a congressional committee, he had believed a small contingent of Americans could "rally the fast-retreating South Korean forces."[10] Task Force Smith was an armed marionette, lowered onto the stage of battle as a kind of *deus ex machina,* to frighten the credulous North Koreans in the audience and give heart to the South Koreans.

As his troops settled into a nearby bivouac, Smith and several of his officers jeeped up the main highway out of Taejon, along the road army engineers called Route 1. The jeeps bumped over deep pits in its gravel surface and skittered sideways through the mud. Because of the rains, the shallow roadbed had turned into a thick gumbo gravy. The road was single-tracked and tortuously curved. Speeding trucks had obliterated most of it. It was rutted and bumpy, puddled from the rain.

With the South Korean retreat turning into a rout, Smith and his staff had to fight a current of humanity: refugees bent beneath heavy bundles of household wares; South Korean soldiers, some dragging rifles, some unarmed; vehicles of every description—old Japanese vans, American two-and-a-half-ton trucks, motorcycles, automobiles, bicycles, yellow buses, tractors, jeeps, wheelbarrows. Trains hurtled by, civilians and soldiers hanging fearfully to their tops. Wounded troops next to the highway cried for help—and were ignored.

All these refugees were not running from "tyranny" or toward "freedom," as American politicians were wont to insist; most were only attempting to stay clear of the steamroller of war, flitting ahead of its mindless violence like insects rushing about as the rumble of giant footsteps approached. Months later, when American forces advanced northward, refugees rushed ahead of *them*. (Sometimes the last half-century seems to stream past in a haunting montage of contorted oriental faces, flickering in smoky black and white like a silent newsreel.)

Off Route 1 lay a Sargasso Sea of hundreds of dead and abandoned vehicles. Some had been strafed by the planes of one side or another and lay pitted and blackened from fire. Some were simply stuck in the mud, surrounded by the narrow gouges in the earth men make when they try to push cars and trucks out of wet ground. Some vehicles had apparently run out of gas or had been stopped by incomprehensible mechanical difficulties. All of them, symbols of the twentieth century, lay useless along the highway, the skeletal remains of war's flash fire.

Along the eighty miles Smith and his men drove, the Korean landscape also sprouted tiny hamlets, clusters of shabby huts with straw-thatched roofs. About every dozen miles lay a genuine, if unassuming, city: Chichiwon, Shinan, Pyongtaek. A railroad track, connecting these towns, meandered back and forth across the highway like a snake. Eventually, they arrived at a place called Osan.

Korea is as wrinkled as an unmade bed. Scrubby hills bulge in puffy protuberances, and sharp ridges crisscross in jagged moonscapes. Later on, American soldiers made a joke about it. They said if someone ironed Korea flat, it would cover the world.

Smith was looking for a spot where he and his men might

halt the flow of the North Korean advance. He searched for a spot where the hills, the highway, and the railroad all came together. He looked for a place to lay an ambush. Two miles north of Osan he found what he wanted. Here the railroad tracks drew several hundred yards back from the road. Between the tracks and the highway jutted two breastlike hills. From their tops you not only had an excellent view of all sides, but you could also see almost all the way to Suwon, eight miles to the north, where Smith had heard the North Koreans were. He decided to make his stand here.

When he returned to Taejon, however, General Church ordered him to divide his force into two parts, putting half at Pyongtaek on Route 1 and the other half at Ansong twelve miles east. The reason was simple. West of Pyongtaek was an estuary of the Yellow Sea where UN ships could patrol; east of Ansong rose a series of mountains which continued almost all the way to the Sea of Japan. The plain between the estuary and the mountains—from Pyongtaek to Ansong—was a bottleneck. The Inmun Gun would squeeze through here. Task Force Smith's job was to make itself a temporary cork in the bottleneck.

That night Smith and his men once again boarded waiting trains. Several hours later they arrived at their positions, and dug in.

The vast American military machine creaked slowly into action. Harry Truman had pushed the button and its levers and gears and pulleys turned—slowly at first then faster and faster. Preparations designed for the eventuality of military conflict were ready. A decade of war and quasi-war had forced military thinkers into some semblance of planning, and their blueprints were drawn.[11]

In strategic American areas around the world guards carefully watched for saboteurs. Locks and dams throughout the Midwest of the United States were suddenly closed to sightseers; all army and naval bases shut their doors to the public; military forces at the Panama Canal, Alaska, and Pearl Harbor went on modified alert. At air bases in Japan, Guam, and Okinawa planes took off and landed every few seconds. (One plane flew over Seoul and dropped leaflets saying that Americans were on their way. "Be steadfast," the leaflets exclaimed in MacArthurian rhetoric. "Be calm. Be courageous. Resist firmly. Together we shall drive the aggressor from your territory.")

The first casualty reports trickled in: Two airmen were killed in a plane crash; eleven others died when a C-54 transport went down. Families in Warren, Arkansas, and Kalamazoo, Michigan, mourned. A lady in Chicago wrote a poignant letter to her newspaper expressing a mother's melancholy. President Truman, she sighed, "doesn't know the anguish, terror, heartache the word 'war' brings to folks with boys in the family—this generation has been long suffering: war, war, war, depression—it isn't right."[12]

Veterans made wry jokes about getting their old uniforms altered to fit their new, somewhat bulgier, bodies. Rumors spread about "secret orders" and "alerts." In New York City a story made the rounds that the state's National Guard was about to be called; the switchboard of the *New York Times* lit up. In Los Angeles a pretty seventeen-year-old jumped to her death from an overpass. She felt despondent because she thought her boyfriend, an ex–army corporal, might be recalled into service.[13]

As the military lurched into action, American civilians reacted in various ways. The nation was (and would remain for the duration) schizophrenic about this war.

In Madison Square Garden thousands cheered speakers who stated that "aggressive war abroad—and that's what we're in—means fascism at home." A few days later, about four hundred people attending a "Hands Off Korea" rally in upper Manhattan heard Paul Robeson tell them that "we want no war." On a commune in Glen Garden, New Jersey, a young man named David Dellinger, his wife, and three others announced a two-week hunger strike which they hoped might arouse the world to end the war.

Such reactions were unusual. Most of the nation ignored them. Neither pacifists nor leftists had any large basis of support.

American blue collar workers patriotically (and blindly) supported their flag. The Switchmen's Union, which had recently struck a number of western railroads, ended its strike when the National Mediation Board appealed to the workers to return to their jobs for the war effort. Electrical workers canceled a six-day strike at the Ingersoll Rand Company in Phillipsburg, New Jersey. The company made pumps, five of which were vital to the new aircraft carrier *Philippine Sea*. The Ingersoll Rand workers fixed the pumps—and went on strike again.

Union men recognized that war was often lucrative. On July 1 the Pacific Maritime Association signed an agreement by which their men received bonus pay for civilian service in Korean waters. Not only did each man get a $10,000 life insurance policy and double pay for merchant marine work in the "war zone," but he also received a $100 bonus if his vessel happened to enter a port under attack and $125 for each bombing raid the ship suffered.

Union leaders who refused to support their government's actions during these early days of the war often came into conflict with their men. Even Harry Bridges, union chief extraordinary, a leader who was genuinely loved by many of his men, had problems. Early in the Korean crisis, before the United States actually entered the civil war, one local of his organization—the International Longshoremen's and Warehousemen's Union—wanted to give blanket support to all future governmental action on the matter. When Bridges proposed that the ILWU ask for UN arbitration instead, one of his workers shouted at him: "Our country is at war! Either you support your country or you're a goddamn traitor who ought to be locked up!"[14]

The economy surged upward, beginning a short, violent inflationary spiral, one of the worst in American history. Stocks rose, the job rate was high, and industrial expansion churned ahead, partly in anticipation of government orders. Housewives began panic-buying. They remembered the shortages of World War II and did not want to be caught without flour or meat or coffee. Grocery stores in Ohio had to ration sugar. In several parts of the country automobile tires sold out in a few hours.

The economy leveled off within a couple of weeks, but it accelerated again in August and then soared for months. It would not reach such inflationary proportions again until the early 1970s.

In general, American society took the war in stride. Hollywood, as always, accepted the situation with equanimity. On June 28 (before the United States had really entered the war) the Title Registration Bureau of the Motion Picture Association of America announced it had already received five hand-delivered titles from movie producers: "Korea," "South Korea," "Crisis in Korea," "Formosa," and "Indo-China." Elsewhere in Hollywood, few seemed to care about the war and things went on as usual. One motion picture company handed out a publicity release stating that the All-American football player (and later Supreme Court justice) Byron "Whizzer" White was about to make his movie debut. In Chicago, audiences—somewhat reduced by the advent of television—saw such pictures as *Father of the Bride, Annie Get Your Gun, Samson and Delilah,* the Marx Brothers in *Love Happy,* and Esther Williams swimming and smiling her way through *Duchess of Idaho.* Chicago moviegoers also saw a plethora of westerns: intelligent ones like Gregory Peck's *The Gunfighter;* utter trash like *Commanche Territory,* a witless saga of a heroic, if slightly moronic, Jim Bowie.

Many Americans did not go to the movies that week. On this Fourth of July holiday much of the nation inexorably pressed toward the sea. Toward sand and sun. Toward fun.

While Brad Smith was surveying the hills near Osan, Americans by the millions vacationed furiously in their usual state of kinetic frenzy. July Fourth fell on a Tuesday that year, which meant that most people took Monday off and had an extra-long weekend. The weather was flawless over much of the nation. Sunday the sky above the eastern seaboard was blue and crystalline. Temperatures stayed high; humidity was low. Coney Island undulated with the raw, parboiled flesh of New Yorkers impatiently determined to tan their pasty bodies in a hurry. Traffic jams became immense, setting awesome local records. Cars waited as long as six hours to cross the Delaware River Bridge.

Even in Europe Americans celebrated their country's one hundred and seventy-fourth birthday. In Paris Americans drank wine toasts in overpriced bistros and drunkenly waved tiny replicas of Old Glory. During the Korean War's first days, several hundred United States citizens returned home, but after these initial nervous flutters subsided almost all the 45,000 Americans in France remained to enjoy themselves. The French National Tourist Office proudly announced that tourism had not been affected by war jitters.

England, also about to be involved in this war, seemed to feel the same holiday atmosphere, perhaps because of the unusually fine weather there. Wimbledon had one of the biggest crowds in its history; airlines carrying passengers from England to the Continent added extra flights; Clement Attlee went to his country estate.

Moscow was at the height of its summer social season. Embassies vied with each other over which could give the most glittering party. Each night the diplomatic corps dressed up in black tie and surrounded itself with a sea of bare shoulders and an aura of expensive perfume. In honor of July Fourth, Alan G. Kirk, United States ambassador to the Soviet Union, gave the biggest ball seen in Russia since World War II. Moscow's first jazz band played a number of decadent bourgeois tunes. The affair was well attended by jovial Russians despite the unpleasantness of a few days earlier, when the Soviet government had formally denounced the United States for dropping potato bugs on East Germany. (The accusation, following a similar East German protest, probably resulted from a crop failure in the Russian zone. Three weeks earlier East Germany had had to suffer the humiliation of buying 50,000 tons of surplus American potatoes.)

American gaiety that week was not the forced, smiling-through-the-agony, we-who-are-about-to-die kind. But neither was the nation totally thoughtless, completely without care. The *New York Times* reported an air of anxiety among people waiting at terminals. Travelers with portable radios often sat quietly listening to broadcasts of the latest news; sometimes a small crowd huddled around them trying to absorb the meaning of the few wisps of information announcers gave out. The sale of newspapers was markedly up. The patriotic drone of Fourth of July speeches seemed more somber than usual.

Governmental activity slowed but did not stop. Most congressmen were home greasing their fingers with barbecued chicken and political neighborliness, but Washington politics continued. Joe McCarthy was especially frenetic. He attacked Dean Acheson for the war: "American boys are dying in Korea," he said dramatically if prematurely (for none had yet arrived in the battle zone). As he saw it, the cause of the Korean War was that "a group of untouchables in the State Department [had] sabotaged" Congress's Korean aid program. He deduced that the State Department harbored "Communists or worse." In his hyperbolic fashion he called the hearings held by Senator Millard E. Tydings of Maryland (which had been a poor attempt to investigate some of his other charges at the State Department) "the most fantastic exhibition I have ever seen put on." Finally, he ominously announced he now had four full-time investigators in the United States (plus another full-time investigator in Europe) and "help from some of my friends."

On June 30 Harry Truman joined 46,634 Boy Scouts from all forty-eight states, several territories, and nineteen other countries at Valley Forge in their annual scout jamboree. He gave them an uninspired speech about "freedom" without mentioning Korea. Whereupon, he drove to the Philadelphia Navy Yard and boarded the presidential yacht, *Williamsburg*. Darkness settled in as he arrived, and one reporter noted that he seemed tense and weary. His daughter, Margaret, had already come from New York, and she and Charlie Ross, the president's press secretary and warm friend, were his only companions (other than the ship's large staff and dozens of reporters aboard the U.S.S *William M. Wood,* the escort destroyer following the presidential boat at a discreet distance).

As usual he was amazingly resilient. Next morning at seven he was standing on the yacht's bridge as it weighed anchor. Every so often during the day he scanned news reports from Korea but they offered little new information. Fighting between North and South Koreans was in a momentary lull. Task Force Smith had not yet arrived in the battle zone. Charlie Ross telephoned reporters on the destroyer that the president was relaxing and that he had received no official communications from either diplomatic or military advisers. Like many a soldier before battle, the president now found that his chief job was waiting. So he relaxed.

About ten that morning he felt lonely and woke Margaret up. The two stood close together by the railing and greeted people on a swarm of pleasure boats which spun around them. The president of the United States, having just involved his country in a war in which millions would die, smiled and waved at hundreds of surprised boaters. The warm sun beat down, not a cloud in the sky, and grinning

Americans beeped their boat horns, shouted halloos, and waved at their president while his yacht slowly sailed into Chesapeake Bay and left them. For a moment awareness of Korea must have receded from Truman's mind. For a few hours he was merely another weekend tourist on a borrowed boat, the yachting cap jaunty on his head.

CHAPTER TEN

To
Osan

We are going forward to meet the enemy. . . .

—General George B. Barth
(July 4, 1950)

JUST BEFORE DARK the *Williamsburg* anchored in the lower Potomac off Blackiston Island, a favorite spot of Truman's. It remained there all night and much of the next day. Not until midafternoon did it return to Washington.[1]

The president returned to Blair House, where one of his first visitors was Frederick J. Lawton, director of the budget. They discussed the economy in general, and more specifically how the war might affect the budget. They came to no conclusions beyond the obvious fact that it would considerably complicate Lawton's bookkeeping.

All was quiet in Washington, but across the world the intricate oriental fabric was unraveling. In Southeast Asia the French, using newly arrived American money and weapons, increased their pressure on the rebel forces; they announced they would soon demolish them. Ho Chi Minh sent a plaintive Fourth of July greeting to the United States, a message of "sincere admiration and fraternity," pleading with Americans to condemn French efforts in Indochina.[2]

In Peking Mao was apparently nervous. The United States was now in Korea, just a few hundred miles from that city. The French were in Indochina, the British were in Hong Kong, and Chiang Kai-shek was of course on Formosa. Mao seemed surrounded. The recent American decisions might signal a general attack on China. Part of Mao's forces headed toward the border between Manchuria and Korea; other divisions moved toward the Indochinese border; even others maneuvered near Hong Kong. Mao obviously wanted to be prepared for any eventuality.

On Formosa about 30,000 Kuomintang troops traveled by train toward the island's northern port of Keelung. Chiang Kai-shek offered their services to Truman and MacArthur. When the Seventh Fleet had moved into position between Formosa and the mainland, Chiang's tenuous status improved. Within a day or so Formosan currency rose 20 percent in relation to the American dollar. Confident now of his present position, Chiang could give his services in Korea. Such an action might help recoup his prestige, place him near Manchuria in case this Korean crisis burst into World War III, and allow him to get some troops of questionable loyalty off Formosa. Truman was inclined to use Chiang's troops but apparently Acheson talked him out of it.[3]

In Japan convoys of trucks and jeeps rushed around, sirens wailing. High-ranking officers double-timed in and out of the Dai Ichi building. The Japanese government, following MacArthur's explicit orders, accelerated attacks on domestic leftists. On June 26 it banned *Akabata,* the major Communist newspaper; five days later it closed down sixty-seven other publications, many, perhaps most of which, were party organs. Japanese police raided a Korean Communist student league in Tokyo and confiscated its anti-American pamphlets. American MPs arrested a number of people in Yokohama for passing out handbills asking dock workers not to load arms for Korea. The Americans charged them with "obstructing the occupation." MPs in the same city arrested a Japanese worker because someone heard him brag he could destroy a massive amount of ammunition with a single well-placed grenade. He was, the official report stated, "found to be a Red."[4]

Meanwhile in Korea, fighting between North and South slowed. After Seoul fell to the Northern army, the victors organized workers' and students' councils. Many of the city's middle class were frightened but most of its population accepted the new situation with bovine equanimity: Cows do not generally care whose hands milk them.

But the North Koreans were confused. Like Napoleon triumphant in Moscow fruitlessly waiting for the tsar's emissaries to accept his terms, they had won a military victory but the political plum did not fall to them. They had hoped a rapid and victorious probe would crumble Syngman Rhee, and that dissatisfied elements in South Korea (including the majority of politicians) would rally to them. Apparently Rhee had destroyed most of those who might have offered support to North Korea. Opponents of his who remained, while they might differ with the tyrannical old patriot over many matters, supported the same basic social philosophy he did. They might not like him, but they liked the North Korean regime less. Also, North Korea had not counted on America's entrance into this civil war.

Pyongyang radio announced the mobilization of all men and women between eighteen and thirty-six. The motherland needed help. But such exhortations were only drumbeating meant to stir patriotic blood—untrained civilians could have no real effect on this war. What North Korea needed was speed, speed, speed. If she could control all Korea before the Americans became too involved, the United States (which, she assumed, was a rational country) might decide to withdraw.

The Inmun Gun brought more gasoline, ammunition, and other supplies down to the Han River and began to build new bridges across it. As Task Force Smith waited at Ansong and Pyongtaek, the North Koreans gathered their energies for the onslaught.

MacArthur's official communiqué for July 2 said: "There was some increase in enemy activity south of the Han River but not much."

Each day elements of the Twenty-fourth Division funneled into Taejon and Pusan. General Dean arrived and took over from Church, who was reduced to deputy commander. American reporters in Korea were pleased. They preferred Dean's straightforward, candid attitude and his tough confidence to Church's phlegmatic aura, which they considered sluggishness rather than calmness.[5]

Dean was a ruddy-faced, brawny man, six feet tall and two hundred pounds of beef, made fairly firm by calisthenics and constant walking. He was a grizzled, crew-cut, self-confessed "physical fitness crank."[6] (Within a few weeks, after personally attacking a tank with a bazooka at close range, he was cut off behind his lines and captured. His reminiscences of his three years in captivity prove him intelligent and sensitive.)

The Fifty-second Field Artillery Battalion was a segment of William Dean's division.[7] On June 30 it was alerted to fly to Korea from Itazuke air base, but the rain that had stalled Smith and his men in Japan had forced the artillery to go by sea. (The twelve-hour voyage must have been hellish. One report described a seventy-mile-an-hour gale in the area.[8]) Lieutenant Colonel Miller O. Perry commanded the battalion. He was a firm, shrewd soldier, about to be one of the heroes of America's first engagement with the enemy. Normally a taciturn man, something in his steely, pale blue eyes indicated what his West Point yearbook called a "bulldog determination."

Meanwhile, American planes threw themselves into action. Errors were inevitable. Even American ground troops had difficulty distinguishing North from South Koreans. Pilots whizzing over poorly mapped terrain with orders to stop the "enemy" were bound to make mistakes. (The only decent maps available were based on a Japanese survey taken between 1918 and 1932. Pilots flying from Japan had few, if any, topographical maps. Sometimes they only saw a sketch map of their target just before they left.) Few Americans felt affection for Koreans, and pilots were often less discriminating than they should have been. Countless civilians (both Northern and Southern) were slaughtered by trigger-happy airmen. The pilots sometimes even shot up Americans. A newspaperman calculated that of the fifteen war correspondents who died in this war, seven were killed by the air force. [9]

The results of this confusion were often disastrous. American pilots attacked a column of thirty ROK trucks, killing two hundred South Korean troops. An American officer working with a ROK unit said he was attacked by "friendly" aircraft five times in one day. He wrote an acquaintance, "The fly boys really had a field day: They hit friendly ammo dumps, gas dumps, the Suwon air strip, trains, motor columns, and KA (Korean Army) Hq." [10] Four Australian planes blew up an ammunition train heading *north* to supply ROK units. Nine boxcars of vital ammunition were destroyed. Task Force Smith was nearby, and a sergeant from Kentucky was wounded in the foot. [11] A private from Illinois wondered, "What kind of screwy war is this?" [12]

At Taejon, Dean and Church tensely examined a large wall map and talked about military strategy. They concluded that Task Force Smith should advance farther north to make room for more elements of the Twenty-fourth Division coming up from Pusan. As Dean and Church were talking, General George B. Barth, in command of the division's artillery, arrived at headquarters. Dean ordered him to go up the highway as his personal representative to see what was happening. Barth took two jeeps and a translator named Lieutenant Colonel Yim. [13]

Brad Smith and Miller Perry, meanwhile, drove from Pyongtaek to Osan to make a reconnaissance of the terrain. [14]

Rain. A light mist in the air. You huddle yourself up under your poncho; you pull your chin into your neck and your head into your shoulders—and still driblets of water find the secret crevices and maliciously tickle down your back. Your boots become heavy; the sodden khaki of your pants rubs your knees raw. The coarse, red earth of Korea becomes a tomato paste, becomes a viscous, gummy substance sucking lustfully at your feet and exhausting your legs beyond endurance.

As day eddied into darkness, American troops picked themselves up, hoisted their weapons, and moved north.

Smith commandeered trucks for his men. He discovered that finding them was relatively easy, getting Korean drivers was more difficult. Refugees and military stragglers oozed south past Pyongtaek carrying stories of those pitiless tanks. The battle above them, they said, was a meat grinder.

Even locomotive engineers refused to move their trains north. An American said, "They would bolt southward at the slightest provocation with train loads of ammunition and supplies for the front line troops. This situation became so serious that it was necessary to place armed guards aboard each engine until the train was actually ready to move." [15]

Five hundred and forty Americans. About a hundred vehicles of various sorts, toting howitzers, C rations, gasoline, radios, toilet paper, water, bandages, and ammunition for rifles, machine guns, mortars, bazookas, and heavy artillery; also hand grenades, rope, shovels, maps, and photographs of mothers, fathers, and favorite dogs, and of girl friends, wives, mooses, and whores in various graphic and gymnastic poses; also pencils and blankets, tents and knives, even a few secret bottles of liquor. The American army on the move. It was only a small unit heading into battle, so it traveled light. It could leave behind the electricians and barbers, cooks and bakers, gravediggers, doctors, policemen, clerks, and the thousands of men who ran the army's movie projectors, cleaned its laundry, flattened its roads, and manipulated the incredible variety of parts and paraphernalia of modern warfare.

By the time they were assembled it was nearly midnight. Rain clouds hung low, fogging the night. Since they were under blackout conditions the trucks moved slowly, with only an occasional sick yellow light to pierce the darkness. The twelve-mile trip through the murk took almost three hours.

Inside the trucks echoed the sounds of men going to war: the clink of canteens, the creak of leather and canvas and cotton; the grunting, the porcine belches, snores, and atavistic breakings of wind; the soft murmur of whispered conversations; the deep growl of heavy vehicles in low gear.

Outside, among the torrent of Koreans coursing past, sandaled feet shuffled quietly through the mud. Perhaps a baby's cry split the night, but if so, a mother's hand or breast soon muffled it. Two nations sliding by each other on the narrow gravel road.

General Barth, Dean's representative, arrived at Pyong-taek just as Smith was leaving. Together they drove north following the trucks.

They came across some ROK engineers setting demolition charges on a bridge. Through his interpreter, Colonel Yim, Barth tried to tell them not to blow it up. "We are going forward to meet the enemy and don't intend to return," he said. "We want the bridges to speed our supplies and reinforcements." The engineers were unimpressed. Finally, Barth got out of his jeep, grabbed the boxes of dynamite, and threw them into the stream. He never considered the possibility that the bridge would have to be blown soon to prevent North Korean tanks from using it. As he later admitted, "No thought of retreat or disaster entered our minds."[16]

The line of vehicles, stretching four or five miles along Route 1, trundled slowly past Osan during the night. The village, a small collection of huts and shacks, clustered where the highway and the railroad tracks came together. Most of its citizens were gone now. The tiny houses lay bare and vacant, waiting to be ravished. The peasants who lived here were gone now—gone somewhere down the road. Some would eventually come back and find their homes demolished. But they would still have the land. They had outlasted conquerors and armies before. They would be back.

It was about three in the morning when the Americans arrived. Now they had to unload the equipment, set the 105-mm. howitzers into position, and dig their foxholes and their trenches.

The men became winded from the immediate task of moving heavy objects, from stumbling over unseen rocks in the dark; they were also weary beyond belief from a week of constant movement. They had been in motion since June 28—the day their outfits had gone on alert. From bases in Japan they had traveled by truck and train and plane and boat for day after day. They had, of course, napped along the way, relaxing their bodies and closing their eyes, sleeping in brief awkward moments like soldiers everywhere. But they were never able to sleep for long. During the past two days they had expected an attack momentarily, and even naps became unusual. By this time some of them drooped from weariness, dragging themselves from place to place in yawning stupor. Tiredness itself became an enemy. Eyes were red-rimmed, spongy knees buckled at unexpected moments, and fingers were so clumsy cigarettes became difficult to hold and light. One man saw an officer fall asleep while giving commands.[17]

Despite their exhaustion they prepared for battle. Artillerymen concealed some trucks behind a wall of houses just north of Osan; in a few hours these vehicles would save a number of their lives. A few hundred yards up the highway was a narrow trail. Using two jeeps in tandem to pull the guns off the road, Colonel Perry placed four of his five "stubby" howitzers in a slight gully amid some bushes.

Half a mile north Perry placed his last howitzer, and he gave this one his best ammunition, six antitank rounds.

In Japan most available artillery ammunition consisted of high-explosive shells, what the military referred to as HE rounds. These performed excellently against infantry; they were capable of decapitating, castrating, mutilating, amputating, blinding, disfiguring, and disemboweling.

But they were almost useless against modern tanks; they exploded into steel fragments which bounced off a tank's thick hide. As early as June 29, in light of the successes North Koreans were having against the ROK army during the war's first hours, Bud Miley, a major general commanding Fort Bragg, North Carolina, wrote Matthew Ridgway that he would like authorization to try an experiment. "I want to shoot at one of our medium tanks," he declared, "and I want to be inside of it at the time of testing." He wanted to find out, he said, what effect a high-explosive round would have on people inside a tank. "I will guarantee that no injury will occur to any personnel, including myself."[18]

The Inmun Gun had Soviet-made, "medium" sized, T-34 tanks. Because of their extremely broad tracks, they had what military experts call excellent "flotation," that is, they did not easily sink into boggy soil. As a result, they were fairly maneuverable on the muddy roads of Korea. The T-34 was fast and had a relatively low profile. It would be very difficult to stop.

As Perry's artillery regiment was leaving Japan, the battalion ammunition officer issued it his total supply of eighteen "high explosive antitank" (HEAT) shells. HEAT shells, according to an army manual, "can penetrate in excess of 10 inches" of armor.[19] When they hit a tank's side at just the right angle, thousands of tiny metal shards burst inside and swarm about; they create a deadly holocaust for any occupants. The eighteen HEAT rounds were divided three ways, so "A" Battery, the regimental section commanded by Miller Perry, got only six.

Incredible boobery marked this whole expedition. Once the decision had been made to send troops, the United States should have provided them with available minimal necessities. To send underarmed men against a superior foe is not only inane, it borders on the criminal. To assume your troops do not need adequate protection because they face an oriental force is blatant, racist stupidity. Acting tough does not make an army invincible. It is like a junior high football coach exercising his team in 95-degree heat or a steady downpour—to "toughen them up."

The infantry, fanned out across a mile of Korean landscape, was a thousand yards in front of the first howitzer. On the left flank, across the highway to the west, Smith positioned a rifle platoon atop a knob. On the east bank of the road were the two breastlike knolls, each about a hundred feet high. Smith split most of the rest of his men into two groups and put half on each hill. He also placed a tiny remnant one hundred yards to the rear—to somehow prevent his little force from being outflanked.

Several volunteers from Perry's artillery unit joined Smith, providing him with four more machine guns and four additional bazooka teams. Not far behind his riflemen Smith arranged his mortars and recoilless rifles. The outfit was as ready as it would ever be.

One artilleryman worriedly asked what would happen if tanks burst through the infantry. "Don't worry," an arrogant trooper told him "they will never get back to you."

An artillery sergeant later sighed, "Everyone thought the

enemy would turn around and go back when they found out who was fighting."

(During the night, South Korean soldiers, perhaps as many as one thousand, stopped just south of the artillery. They had been fighting a losing battle for days. They were brave but at this moment they were skittish. They watched to see how the soldiers of the United States would do.[20] A lieutenant recalled his feelings about the ROK troops near him. "We paid no attention to them. We figured they were not regular soldiers and had not fought tanks before."[21])

What incredible hubris! Shades of General Thomas Gage and the colonial militia; shades of Generals Westmoreland, Taylor, and Abrams, and Messrs. Kennedy, Rusk, Bundy, and McNamara and those skinny little Vietnamese in black pajamas. On July 5, 1950, the United States government and army in their vast nationalistic (and probably racist) confidence had positioned 540 troops—most of them young, green, and soft—directly in the path of a proud, victorious North Korean army of 40,000. Western civilization, such as it was, was about to receive an oriental blow to its ego, to its morale, and to its centuries-old tradition of superiority over the wogs and the fuzzy-wuzzies and the gooks of the world.

Dead soldiers. (George Silk, TIME-LIFE Picture Agency,© Time Inc.)

A grief-stricken infantryman whose friend has been killed is comforted by an-other soldier. In the background a corpsman fills out casualty tags. (U. S. Army photo)

Face of war. (Hank Walker, TIME-LIFE Picture Agency,© Time Inc.)

Flags of the United Nations and the United States over the Dai Ichi Building in Tokyo, General MacArthur's headquarters. (U. S. Army photo)

Major General John H. Church (U. S. Army photo)

John J. Muccio, U. S. ambassador to Korea, and Lieutenant General John Coulter, former deputy commanding general, U. S. 8th Army. (U. S. Army photo)

The Joint Chiefs of Staff meet. Left to right: Admiral Forrest P. Sherman, chief of naval operations; General Omar N. Bradley, chairman, Joint Chiefs of Staff; General Hoyt S. Vandenberg, chief of staff, U. S. Air Force; and General J. Lawton Collins, chief of staff, U. S. Army. (U. S. Army photo)

Two navy wives whose husbands are about to leave. (Ralph Crane, TIME-LIFE
Picture Agency, © Time Inc.)

CHAPTER ELEVEN

Tanks

It may be that tank warfare as we have known it will soon be obsolete.
—Secretary of the Army Frank Pace, Jr.
(June 14, 1950)

DAYLIGHT SLIPPED into Korea and grayed the profiles of taut young American faces.

A soldier recalls, "It was raining to beat hell."[1] Task Force Smith, squatting wetly in their foxholes, water pooling around their boots, test-fired their weapons to make sure they would not jam. Their serpentine ponchos slithered and swished. Wearily, soggily, they ate their C rations. And waited.

The men of the North Korean 107th Tank Regiment devoured their rice, joked quietly, and prepared to move out. They were to lead their Fourth Division south. Just the day before, they had completed the takeover of Suwon and stopped to rest and consolidate their forces.

About seven that morning the tank commanders slid into their vehicles, revved their motors, and squinted down the highway. Very few, if any, knew the United States was in the war. They may have been aware a small military unit stood in their way.

On June 25, two weeks earlier, the day war began, they had led the attack on Seoul itself. They were good soldiers with excellent mobile equipment. They had had a superb plan. Like Hannibal's troops against the Romans at Cannae, like the Germans in both world wars, the army of the Democratic People's Republic was designed for rapidity. Whenever they bumped against opposition, they spread out to envelop and surround it. They executed their orders with precision and courage. An American military leader soon wrote about his North Korean opponent: "His infantry was well-trained, physically tough, and exceedingly aggressive. The tactics used were well planned and well executed."[2]

Sergeant Kim Chin Ok of the Inmun Gun was twenty-one years old. He had been in the army a little over a year. His specialty was building bridges and repairing roads. He was a sergeant because he was the only man in his company with more than five years' education; he had six. He didn't like officers. He thought they were selfish. They always ate three meals a day, while enlisted men like him only got to eat once or twice. On the morning of July 5, 1950, he and his engineers' unit were in Suwon facing south.[3]

Using binoculars to peer through the rain and the haze, Smith saw some movement up near Suwon a little after seven. He told his men to be ready. Minutes ticked slowly by. Soon others next to him could see tank silhouettes along the road, ominous, beetle-like lumps crawling toward them. Lieutenant Phil Day, with "C" Company, felt surprise that the North Korean force looked more powerful, more organized than he had been led to believe. He later admitted that he was "amazed and apprehensive to say the least."[4] The reactions of the rest of the troops varied. Some accepted their role calmly, phlegmatically; others were cocky and could hardly wait to emulate the heroes in all those war movies they had seen—William Bendix, John Wayne, Robert Walker. Some, like Phil Day, were jittery, as worried that they might fail in their duty as they were about dying.

Others were sullen, resentful at having to be there. (About two weeks earlier, the regiment had sent six or eight enlisted men back to the United States to be discharged for incompetence, but when war started the army returned them. Most of them behaved cravenly at Osan.[5])

In 1950 Americans prized bravery in battle above all human characteristics: above compassion, above goodness, above decency. The soldiers along the road knew this. Their mettle was about to be tested, not only in the eyes of their comrades, but in their own as well. How they performed in the next few hours might determine their self-images for the rest of their lives. To some the experience would be exhilarating, to a few shattering, to others fatal.

In the United States it was still the evening of July Fourth. At the same moment American howitzers began to fire in Korea, cheerful volunteer firemen on a baseball diamond in Ridgefield, Connecticut, shot rockets and roman candles into the sky, and hundreds of watching children gasped and cheered. In New York City adolescents listened to the latest popular songs on WIN's program "Music in the Night." Perhaps they heard Dinah Shore croon about "those dear hearts and gentle people who live in my home town," or Bing Crosby syncopate his way through "Chattanooga Shoe Shine Boy." Older folks might be listening to the program "America's Town Meeting," whose topic for the night was the question "Is the Fair Deal destroying individual responsibility?" Television viewers watched "Her Nibs" Miss Georgia Gibbs sing on the Ed Wynn show or Ray McKinley's orchestra spark the "Cavalcade of Bands," or Ted Mack smile benignly upon the sweating contestants of the "Original Amateur Hour." One station that night presented a "Miss Television, 1950" contest, and another showed a woman's wrestling match in Bayonne, New Jersey, pitting Millie Stafford against Mars Bennett.

Somewhere, someone turned on the victrola to play Peggy Lee's latest number, a song which almost seemed to describe this existential moment—"When the World Was Young."

Miller Perry had sent a small team up with the infantry to be the artillery's eyes. At about eight o'clock his observation officer called back to him, "Target of four tanks. Request fire."[6]

General Barth had been with Brad Smith all night, watching Smith's troops get into position. As it was getting light—just before the tanks hove into sight—he went a mile back down the highway to the howitzers. He later remembered the time was 8:16 when the number two howitzer fired its first round. Then the rest of the artillery blasted away at the tanks, still two miles in the distance.

The infantry on the knolls heard the muzzle blast of the guns behind them and the whistle of shells overhead, and could see the explosions around the tanks. They observed that all this had no effect on the machines lumbering at them. Through the smoke the men could see that the tanks were not only unscathed, but seemed unconcerned. The machines stayed in perfect column and merely shrugged the howitzers' blasts off their massive metal shoulders.

General Barth, an experienced artillery man, immediately saw the implications: The Americans had failed in their primary objective, for the North Koreans had not retreated in panic in the face of United States firepower and determination. Previously, General Church had optimistically stated, "All we need is some men up there who won't run when they see tanks." He had been wrong. Barth sped back toward Pyongtaek to warn the men there that enemy tanks were coming at them. He wanted to make sure they were prepared.

The colonel of this Thirty-fourth Regiment, Red Ayers, sat in what one observer called "a tiny thatched hut sur-

rounded by a sea of mud," shared "with a filthy assortment
of chickens, pigs, and ducks."[7] Several reporters arrived at
the grubby headquarters and tried to keep warm with cups
of hot coffee. They were there when Barth arrived. "Enemy
tanks are heading south," he exclaimed. "Get me some
bazooka teams pronto." Then he looked up and saw the startled faces of the journalists and amended his statement.
"Colonel Smith's battalion is forward. We can depend on
him to hold on." But, he added, "if any tanks do get by those
batteries they'll head straight for here."[8]

Barth rolled out a crackling map on the porch floor. "We
must find those tanks and knock hell out of them." He
ordered several bazooka teams to go north by jeep to find
them.[9] (Neither he nor Colonel Ayers told anyone about
their predicament. Hours *later,* one of the regiment's platoon leaders called his men together. He explained that
rumors of a major North Korean army coming at them were
untrue. In a few weeks, he promised, they would be back in
Japan at Sasebo. "You've been told repeatedly," he announced, "that this is a police action, and that is exactly
what it is going to be."[10])

At eleven a headquarters spokesman claimed confidence
that Smith would stop the tanks, but admitted, "I can't say
for sure because . . . we have not heard from them for two
hours."[11] Because of the rain, Smith's radios had only
worked fitfully, and they had finally sputtered and died.

Two young lieutenants began to take a small convoy of
ammunition to the front, but were stopped halfway to Osan
by one of the bazooka teams which had preceded them. The
leader of the team pointed out it was too late. There, in the
road in front of them, was a tank well south of Smith's
position. The group at Osan had obviously been overrun.[12]

A South Korean soldier on horseback, his helmet camouflaged with small sticks and branches poking up at odd angles, his eyes wild, galloped down Route 1. "Tanks! Tanks!

Tanks!" he screamed at the Americans. "Go back!"[13] Those who saw him wondered what had happened to Task Force Smith.

At Osan warriors clashed in ancient tribal rites. Two Neanderthal bands battling for turf.

Soon after Barth left, the North Koreans' tank column passed through the saddle in the road and came under attack from all angles. (Several North Koreans, huddled on the decks of the forward tanks, died instantly. Some of their bodies remained sprawled atop the vehicles, in broadening pools of blood and mucus, but other corpses jolted slowly off and fell into ghastly heaps along the side of the road. They were the first to die at Osan.)

American bazooka teams moved in close to the tanks as they passed. Lieutenant Jim Cox edged up to the highway and fired broadside at them without any effect. From the other side a second lieutenant from Mississippi named Ollie Connor drew within fifteen yards and fired more than twenty rockets, a whole box of shells, directly into them, sparks flying as they hit. His fourth round seemed to damage one tank's treads, and he was moving after another when someone shouted, "Behind you, Lieutenant!" He whirled around just in time to see the machine gun of a third tank rotating toward him. He snapped a shot at it and sprinted into a ditch.[14] Jack Doody, who witnessed Connor's stand, described it as one of the bravest acts he ever saw. But it was not enough. The tanks continued to move. Doody later said, "Rockets hit the tanks in their tracks, turrets, and bodies, and still couldn't stop them."[15]

The two front tanks did halt for some reason—perhaps the bazooka teams had crippled them—and their pause proved fatal. They came under the direct fire of the front howitzer, the gun with the six HEAT rounds. Both tanks began to smoke and pulled off the road to allow the others to pass. A third waddled ahead, fired at the forward howitzer, and destroyed it. Then the remaining T-34s pressed relentlessly on: two more, a clump of four right behind, another cluster, four more, and so on—thirty-one in all. As they drove out of sight, they rode over Smith's communication wire and mangled it. (Since the Americans had assumed they would stop the tanks, they had stretched their lines along the road. Communications with Perry's artillery now faltered and soon stopped altogether. During the next few hours the artillery was isolated.)

As the last tank receded in the distance away from the infantry position—and Smith's men could already hear the thudding of artillery shells and the chatter of machine guns from Perry's outfit—several infantrymen approached the two crippled machines.

One tank burst into flames as they came close, and two Korean soldiers scrambled from the fiery turret with their hands up. They stood there next to their burning vehicle watching the Americans, who in turn examined them warily. Their apparent surrender may have been a trap because suddenly out of the tank popped a third Korean with a burp gun. He pulled the trigger, killing an American machine gunner. (This anonymous American was the first of his country's soldiers to achieve the dubious honor of dying in ground action in this war.)

The Americans turned their guns on all three Koreans and cut them down.

(Nobody on the American side could later recall what happened to the other disabled tank. Jack Doody vividly remembers one man—whose name he cannot recollect—who jumped onto a wounded T-34 and threw a hand grenade down its turret. Presumably this was it.)

Meanwhile, down the road, Perry's howitzers began to fire on the approaching tanks. The North Korean tankmen were confused. They realized a battery of artillery was somewhere in front of them, but scrunched as the tankmen were into their metal wombs, only able to peer through clitoral eye slots, they could not discern it. They paused behind a hillock and scanned the highway ahead. Perry's shrewdness at dragging his guns well off the road now proved valuable, for his guns were virtually invisible. The Koreans could not wait any longer; their orders were to advance as rapidly as possible. Cloud cover would not last forever, and American planes might appear overhead at any moment. One at a time the tanks scuttled down the highway with their hatches closed, firing blindly in all directions. As they swept past the hidden trail, the howitzers shot directly into their flanks. The shells still bounced off.[16]

One tank stopped at the entrance to the path. It was like a dog sniffing a scent, snuffling around it for a while. Then it moved on.

As the first tanks swarmed past, several bazooka teams, one led by Colonel Perry and the other by a sergeant named Ed Eversole, maneuvered close to the road. As Eversole fired a round at a tank, it suddenly revolved its turret toward him. God, he thought, it looks "as big as a battleship."[17] It fired its cannon at him, and the shell sheared off a telephone pole a few feet away. He dove into the muck of a drainage ditch by a rice paddy, so the pole fell harmlessly over him.

One howitzer eventually damaged a tank. After the tanks ahead of it disappeared, Perry sneaked up to it with a Korean interpreter. He whispered instructions to the interpreter, who called to the tankmen to surrender. The North Koreans inside, probably terrified, said nothing. Perry ordered the howitzers to open fire on the tank. Inside, the din must have been horrible, mind-bursting reverberations of clash and clang. After three rounds two Koreans vaulted from the hatch, shooting as they came, one shot hitting Perry in the right leg. They then jumped behind a drainage culvert near the path. Perry sent a squad after them. Small-arms fire riddled the morning and the two Koreans fell dead. (For the rest of the day Perry hobbled about on his wounded leg. He remarked wryly that if he were not so bowlegged he might have had his testicles shot off.[18])

About ten minutes after the first wave of tanks rumbled out of sight, the second appeared, strung out down the highway in haphazard clusters of two and three, like cross-country runners near the end of a race. Some of the artillery crews, realizing they could not stop the tanks, and psychologically unprepared for defeat, panicked and ran away. (Later, such actions became more common. Soldiers would dryly call them "bugging out.") Sergeants and officers, led by a young first lieutenant named Dwain Scott who would receive a Silver Star for this, loaded and fired the guns themselves. The frightened men soon returned to their positions.

This was the first time Americans in Korea literally fled. In running, Americans were doing the same thing they had sneered at their ROK allies for. It should have—but probably did not—make them more sympathetic to the South Korean troops, whose casualty rates would be consistently much higher throughout the war.

As the second set of tanks whizzed by, the 105s stopped one more of them. By ten-fifteen all the rest had disappeared to the south. It was quiet.

The battle's first phase was over. The Americans had destroyed four tanks and damaged three others; they had probably killed two or three dozen of the enemy. In turn the North Koreans had knocked out one howitzer, disabled another, and destroyed all nineteen of the infantry's jeeps along with a great deal of ammunition (which Smith had overconfidently placed just behind his position). As many as twenty American troops were wounded; at least one was dead.

During the brief hiatus after the tanks left, the soldiers

scurried about. Some dug more foxholes and gathered ammunition in piles. Some urinated and defecated in narrow trenches, a few ate C rations. Medics tended the wounded.

The smell of vomit and sweat hung in the air. Flies buzzed softly around the battlefield to gorge on blood.

CHAPTER TWELVE

Defeat

We met vehicles and American PWs. We also saw some American dead.
We found four of our destroyed tanks.

Near Osan there was a great battle.

—Diary of a North Korean soldier
(July 5, 1950)

SMITH SQUINTED through binoculars toward Suwon, his crow's-feet deep with weariness and tension. His arms ached from the weight of the glasses. The tanks, he knew, had only been a preliminary, the steel tip of a battle lance. Before long, infantry would arrive. In rice-paddy terrain tanks are relatively road-bound. They are not quite as dangerous as their clanking, bloated bodies appear. Well-trained infantry, however, can be lethal.

About an hour after the tanks disappeared Smith saw some movement ahead. He stared intently at it. Far in the distance a snakelike object slithered toward him, twisting slowly through convoluted turns and bends in the highway. As Smith scrutinized it, it took substance; it was a North Korean column six miles long. Three tanks led the way, forming a lumbering metal shield. Then came an almost endless line of trucks of various sizes, and behind them shambled thousands of foot soldiers, some dressed in the mustard-colored uniforms of the People's Army, others still wearing the traditional baggy whites of the Korean peasant.

They moved confidently with the nonchalance of successful soldiers on the march, the whole column creeping at the slow pace of the men at the rear. They seemed unaware that they sauntered toward death. Their insouciance is hard to explain; the tanks which had gone by two hours ago should have told them about the American ambush. Apparently their communications were poor or broken.

As the column approached, young GIs (who, a few weeks before, had expected their most hazardous feats to be avoiding venereal disease or crossing streets against Japanese traffic) must have felt a tickle of fear. It was increasingly difficult to view the enemy as some celluloid figures from their childhood—sinister, sneering, yellow men with coke-bottle-bottom glasses and buck teeth, faintly redolent of popcorn, licorice, and tootsie rolls: Saturday matinee evil; evil without harm or pain; evil which dissolves when good guys enter the scene. So many of the American troops were only boys. A few months earlier they had been acned adolescents whose major expressions of machismo had been to humiliate the weakest, most effeminate kid in class or to swagger down the school corridor giving buddies hard whaps on the arm (up near the shoulder).

A hypothetical conversation between two privates at Osan:

FIRST PRIVATE (*gaping at the oncoming line of tens of thousands of the enemy*): "Jesus Christ, look at that!"

SECOND PRIVATE (*softly, almost reverently, as if in church*): "Holy shit. . . ."

What were they like, those American soldiers? An automatic rifleman with the poetic name of Robert Burns was perhaps representative. His mother had died when he was a boy, leaving him the only child of an aging father. He had lived on Stony Island Avenue in Chicago in a rundown, nondescript neighborhood. The romance of military life seemed more exciting then humdrum classes at school, so when he was sixteen he lied about his age and enlisted in the navy. But they sent him home. Back in Chicago he was restless, irritable, and anxious to leave again. At seventeen he joined the army. He was an irrepressible, voluble youth, filled with all the zest a tall, good-looking, dark-haired eighteen-year-old could have. [1]

The North Korean column was about half a mile away, within range of the howitzers, the mortars, and the machine guns, when, according to Smith, his men "threw the book at them." [2] One moment, oblivious North Koreans tramped through the mud of the road, unaware of their enemy. The next instant machine guns stuttered their staccato chatter, mortars belched.

(Colonel Perry's 105s might have wrought terrible damage on the convoy, but his communications malfunctioned again and he did not fire. He had sent a squad to repair the wire, but they were vulnerable targets on the bare road and North Korean small-arms fire forced them back. Again Perry ordered some men up to fix the line, and again they had to retreat. Finally he sent one of his officers out to lay a wire directly across the rice paddies. But by this time the battle was over.)

Even without their artillery, the Americans' first, unexpected assault was devastating. Trucks burst into flames and bodies flew onto the roadway.

How does one describe battle deaths? Cardboard figures do not collapse soundlessly in comic surprise, nor do dying men decline in ketchup-covered, slow-motion, ballet swoons.

Death is not quiet. Sphincter muscles relax in the shock of pain and fear and great swooshes of noxious gases accompany fecal material. Men scream—in the high-pitched shrills of women in labor, in the yip-yipping of run-over dogs, in stunned surprise. Vibrato gagging sounds of retching soldiers detonate in gurgled explosions. Men swear the earthiest expletives of their people, the coarsest, foulest curses that they know. Some men cry, some whimper softly, only a few tumble quietly and do not move.

Nor is death clean and dignified. Shrapnel rips filthy gashes in the abdomen and turns a man's insides out. A soldier has little grandeur when he is cupping his intestines with gory palms or is staring down in horror at his own penis which quivers on the ground, or watching pink bubbles swim over the walls of his own lungs. There is little nobility in aqueous humor drooling across a gray cheek, or artery ends vibrating within a stump, or the stray splinters of teeth and jagged gobbets of flesh strewn amid the carnage.

Combat is not romance. It is vicious ferocity.

As soon as the Americans began to spray them with machine-gun fire, the North Koreans went into action. (A day or so later MacArthur's headquarters in Tokyo released a communiqué accurately describing what happened at Osan. "The American forces were confronted with a resourceful Red commander who skillfully applied frontal pressure with an envelopment."[3]) The frontal pressure came from the three tanks which ground to within two or three hundred yards and began firing right into the American position. While tank fire pinned the GIs down, as many as one thousand North Koreans alighted from trucks and sidled into predetermined patterns. Some moved directly toward the Americans, others deployed into two wings which circled the flanks on either side. The rest of the trucks and the infantry behind them merely waited, as if this were a momentary inconvenience soon to be swept aside.

The North Koreans slithered close. All at once a bugle blew a few eerie notes and a group of them rushed toward the summit. American gunfire drove them back.[4] The charge was only a probing action; the real danger lay on either side. But the bugle blast must have electrified the GIs, few of whom had ever encountered anything like it. (Military forces without adequate modern radio communications find bugles superlative instruments for transmitting messages over relatively short distances. American soldiers in Korea would later learn to correlate bugle notes with danger.)

As tank fire and infantry pressure forced the Americans to concentrate on their front, their adversaries crept onto a high ridge overlooking their left flank. Suddenly the platoon on the west side of the road was threatened with annihilation. Smith realized his predicament and ordered his entire force to move into one central spot, to pull in the perimeters, to draw up into a fist. He sent word to the isolated platoon to edge toward him, and he told Captain Charles Dashner, commander of "C" Company on his right flank, to pull in. Smith's executive officer, Major Floyd Martin, organized the transferral of ammunition to a central location. Martin himself hoisted boxes of ammunition and carried them across open fields. Bullets and shrapnel flew around him as he staggered back and forth.[5]

The Koreans, meanwhile, climbed a high mound on the other side and had Task Force Smith bracketed. Shooting became extremely heavy. (Captain Dashner suggested to Smith that they begin to retreat, at least to the next line of hills. Smith told him no, not right away.[6] Exactly what Smith hoped to accomplish at this point is difficult to say. Perhaps his exhaustion fogged his mind. He should have moved back. His stubborn refusal to do so probably cost a number of lives needlessly.)

Vern Mulligan, a private first-class machine gunner, was firing his weapon when something shot away its tripod. He picked the gun up and laid it on an empty ammunition box. Enemy fire around him intensified. Bullets hit the ammunition box and demolished it. Then six North Koreans popped up near him. Mulligan—filled with battle adrenalin, the elixir of heroes—lifted his machine gun, placed its barrel across his forearm, and opened fire, killing all six.[7]

Smith's unit, under heavy attack for two hours, was running low on ammunition when he finally decided to pull back. As he later said with unintentional irony: "In an obviously hopeless situation, with many casualties, no communication, no transportation, ammo gone, and the enemy tanks now well behind us, I was faced with the decision: What the hell to do?" The answer was simple: "I chose to try to get out."[8]

He had waited too long. Moreover, his withdrawal orders were hasty and fumbling. He had failed to think them through carefully in advance. One platoon never even received them and only discovered it was left behind when a messenger it sent to the command post rushed back to say no one was there. The platoon commander, Lieutenant Carl Bernard, organized what was left of his platoon and took off as fast as he could. For two days he and his men, totally isolated and without any rations, wandered south. Five times they had to skirt North Korean roadblocks. On July 7 Bernard and twelve of his platoon staggered into Chonan. (Perhaps nobody told Perry's artillerymen who had volunteered that morning to stay forward with the infantry, because not one of them returned.[9])

A number of litter cases had to be left behind. "That's the worst part of a deal like that," Brad Smith later groaned, "to leave wounded and dying men yelling for you to help them, and there was no way to help them."[10] An anonymous medic stayed behind. No one knows what happened to him. Two platoon sergeants, veterans of World War II, also stayed. They even refused direct orders to leave. War makes some men hate. It brings out compassion in others. It sometimes reveals a love for one's comrades, a tenderness men often feel toward each other but which they dare not show in civilian life. Both platoon sergeants were taken prisoner. Master Sergeant Vann died in a prison camp in North

Korea; Staff Sergeant Bailey survived and was released three years later. [11]

Six medics, each of whom had served all day as litter bearers, refused to evacuate without taking some wounded with them. Led by a sergeant named Warren Shutter, they put some injured GIs on stretchers, and under continuous fire from mortars, automatic rifles, and the tank cannons they jogged and clambered across rice paddies and over hills to safety. [12]

A lieutenant in the medical corps named Bodie Adams was equally determined. He tried to move his men back to safety but they were kept immobile by fire from a particular machine gun. Finally he crawled on his belly as close as he could to the gun, and from thirty or forty yards away he reared back and somehow threw a hand grenade all the way to the gun. (Maybe it was his pitching arm; he had been the pitcher on the regimental baseball team.) He and his men moved on. [13] Thirty-six medical corpsmen had originally been part of Task Force Smith. A great many did not make it out.

Other acts of courage or bravado marked the retreat. Private First Class Florentin Gonzales (like Vern Mulligan) was a machine gunner. His unit, "B" Company, was the last to leave. The enemy was closing in; many probably would not make it. Like a character out of fiction ("Come and get it, you dirty Krauts!") Gonzales volunteered to stay with his gun to help cover his outfit's withdrawal, most especially that of his buddy, the assistant machine gunner, who was seriously wounded. As his unit was leaving, Gonzales himself was hit, but he kept shooting. His citation for bravery states: "Private First Class Gonzales was last seen to be firing his machine gun when his position was overrun by the enemy." [14]

Another incident can only be credited because it appears within an official report, the typically sodden, stilted, unimaginative prose of a soldier-clerk. A lieutenant, limping to the rear, passed six infantrymen so severely injured they could not move.

"Lieutenant," one of them called, "what is going to happen to us?"

"This is the best I can do for you," the officer muttered as he handed the young man a grenade and walked on. [15]

Some of the slightly wounded moved out with the rest of the battalion but many could not keep up. They fell farther and farther behind, and eventually a few dropped out of sight completely and were never seen again.

Peter Kalischer, a thirty-five-year-old UP reporter, had arrived at Osan that morning just as the battle started. During its height he helped a medical sergeant named David Sutherland dig trenches to protect the wounded. That night, Sutherland back at headquarters rubbed his aching feet, blistered from walking, and explained to reporters that he did not know where their colleague Kalischer was. The last time he had seen him, he said, the journalist was wearing a helmet and was still digging ditches. Sutherland assumed he had been captured. [16]

Two days later, Peter Kalischer hobbled in and told the following story. During the first hours of the retreat, young GIs stumbled through paddies sobbing in fear and exhaustion. A sergeant from Mendon, Illinois, named Allen Palmer was so sick (probably from dysentery) he could not keep up. Kalischer and a captain stopped and rigged a litter for the sergeant. For the next sixty hours the two men carried Palmer, zigzagging to avoid capture. Most of the villages they came to were ghost towns whose inhabitants had fled south. One night they stayed at a farmhouse (along with six ROK soldiers, who were also on the run). They rested and ate a few spoonfuls of rice, then stood up with their litter and kept moving. It was a long two and a half days. [17]

No one later could estimate how many died during the

first part of the withdrawal. An organized retreat is a complicated and tricky maneuver. Students of military history who have studied the campaigns of George Washington, Frederick the Great, or Robert E. Lee know this basic military fact. The skirmish at Osan illustrates it once again. Before the withdrawal, considering they had been facing an overwhelming enemy since almost eight that morning, Smith's casualties were not devastating—most likely only a handful killed and two dozen or more severely wounded. The vast majority of American losses at Osan occurred during the evacuation.

The retreat Smith ordered was supposed to be the classic leapfrog maneuver: One group was slowly to pull back while another guarded its withdrawal; the process would then be reversed, the forward unit moving as the rear unit covered it. But leapfrogging only works when the vaulter becomes the vaultee, when all the frogs in line play the same game so that the last one can leap his fellow amphibians all the way to the rear. But the retreat from Osan became a helter-skelter flight. Men bolted like terrified creatures fleeing a forest fire. Some ran in packs, some alone. They split and came together as geography and other conditions allowed. They dropped weapons, helmets, utensils, belts, anything that might slow them down. At first they darted from rock to rock, but when they came to feculent rice paddies, green with young shoots, they dashed in hoping the muck would hide them.

Young Robert Burns of Chicago made it. He had nothing left by the time he got back to his lines but his boots and his dungarees. He told a reporter how it was. He and another soldier, he said, joined a sergeant, "who guided us out." The three crossed fields, hip-deep in mud. North Korean troops chased them for several miles. Burns admitted he never even fired his gun. He said he tried to shoot it, but when it jammed he threw it away. In the irrationality of total panic he carried his ammunition for a long time before dropping it. "The last thing I threw away," he said, "was my entrenching tool. That was when we had to help a fellow who got wounded in the leg." He felt no shame. He said to a listening reporter from Chicago: "Tell my dad I'm all right. I haven't got a scratch but I'm plenty tired." He had come fifty miles from Osan.[18]

For days the soldiers of Task Force Smith straggled in. They turned up all over southern Korea, many barefoot, their boots tied together by the laces and hanging around their necks.[19]

Some came in bunches, like the sixty-five with Captain Dashner. His unit, "C" Company, was the first one out, and he was able to keep much of it together. A young lieutenant, Harold Dill, organized another group of GIs, some of them wounded, and led them south. They moved for six days behind enemy lines. They arrived hungry, bedraggled—and alive. Sergeant David Columbe, a thirty-four-year-old Sioux Indian, led three others to safety, telling them to play dead whenever the enemy passed.[20] (In those days the army did not teach you what to do if cut off from your own forces; perhaps Sergeant Columbe had received some of his training on the reservation.) Several troopers hiked all the way across the peninsula to the east coast. One of them eventually arrived at Pusan on a Korean sampan.[21]

Some soldiers were captured along the way. Second Lieutenant Jansen C. Cox was part of a group of thirty-six who were southeast of Osan when they were seized the day after the battle. The North Korean army must have considered him a find, for the commanding officer of its Second Division himself interrogated Cox. The Koreans took him to Seoul, interrogated him again, and photographed him along with the rest of his group as kind of a team trophy.[22] North Korean soldiers captured another officer named Captain Ambrose H. Nugent. He had been a member of Perry's Fifty-second Artillery Battalion; he was probably one of the volunteers who fought alongside the infantry. On July 11 Nugent read a 1,000-word statement over North Korean radio. It was one of those dictated pieces of rhetoric, so clumsy they are almost laughable, full of Wall Street warmongers and bloodthirsty American capitalists, the sort of nonsense that makes Communist propaganda look so foolish to Westerners.[23] Exactly why Nugent agreed to read it is unknown, but the North Koreans probably not only threatened his life but told him they would slaughter other American captives as well. Or, maybe he was tortured. If so, it would have been unusual, for North Koreans at that time were not usually torturing American prisoners. (They did, however, execute them. Not long after the war began, the bodies of American soldiers were found, shot in the head, their hands tied or wired behind their backs.) North Korean brutality was like American child-abuse—a result of ignorance, stupidity, and casual, mindless violence, more the result of simple truculence than malevolence.

Not only were North Koreans slightly less bestial than many descriptions of them have portrayed, American prisoners of war were less cowardly than their nation was later willing to admit. Afterward during the 1950s, the United States, in a state of conservative mea culpa, whipped itself raw for its apparent effete weakness. Joe McCarthy was only the center ring of this self-flagellating circle. Mickey Spillane, prussianized crew cuts, "cool" (and years later, "vigah," and probably even President Richard Nixon's constant refrain about how tough he was)—all these symbolized the era's desire for a hairy-chested image. College students in ROTC classes were told and retold how "one-third" of American POWs in the Korean War "ratted." Military instructors emphasized the importance of the Code of Military Justice. ("Just give your name, rank, and serial number.") If you became a prisoner, it was your duty to try to escape.

Somewhere along the way, particularly with the publication of a 1959 best-seller called *In Every War But One* (by

Eugene Kinkead), many Americans concluded that their fighting men in Korea—and therefore perhaps themselves— were weak. Kinkead's piece, originally an extended article in the *New Yorker* magazine, was merely a well-written Sunday supplement, beefed up with pseudo-psychological mumbo jumbo. Unfortunately, many readers believed it. An exhaustive analysis of the actions of American POWs made by an extremely able social psychologist named Albert Biderman, using some of the best scientific techniques, had only limited readership. After one small printing it sank out of sight.[24] Biderman showed that few American soldiers in captivity committed treason. Those who did were not representative of their nation, for they were not a typical group. In general they were less educated, more psychologically alienated, and had lower IQs than the average. (Biderman, incidentally, also destroys the myth of the simplicity of brainwashing.)

Brad Smith decided to try to reach Miller Perry's outfit himself. He had not had any communication with it since morning, since the tanks had charged it. He assumed it was in a shambles, perhaps everyone dead or gone, but he felt obligated to inform anyone still there that he and his men were leaving. He was not optimistic. Perry had only had a few more than 120 men. If the tanks had not destroyed them, certainly the North Korean infantry, already well south of the knolls, would have annihilated such a puny, defenseless group.

As Smith crept through the rice paddies, he suddenly came across the wire party Perry had sent out to reopen lines with the infantry. Together they returned to the howitzers. Smith was astonished. Not only were all four artillery pieces in working order, but only three men were wounded.[25]

When Smith ordered the artillerymen to withdraw, they moved with alacrity. (They had not known the details of the unseen battle in front of them, but their ears, trained to recognize the various sounds of gunfire, had guessed its nature; they had been able to tell that Smith's group was facing a large infantry force and that the Americans were losing.) Now they realized they only had a few minutes before North Korean infantry appeared. Perry's men removed the sights and breech locks from the howitzers. (An artilleryman's dictum is that you almost never abandon your guns, but if you must, dismantle them before you leave.)

Smith and the artillerymen began to maneuver their way south. Just outside Osan they discovered another amazing stroke of luck; the Korean tanks had somehow overlooked the artillery's vehicles. The relieved soldiers clambered aboard. They assumed the tanks were far down the highway toward Pyongtaek, and their plan was to go south until just below Osan, where they could take a road heading east.

As they came around a bend in the highway, not quite out of Osan, they abruptly stumbled upon three enemy tanks. Several North Koreans were standing around nonchalantly smoking cigarettes. Miller Perry, in a marvelous understatement, said that the Americans "retired smartly around their flank." In other words, they spun their jeeps and galloped north again. Neither side fired a shot.

On the north edge of town Smith and Perry discovered a dirt road. They turned in, hoping it would not lead to a dead end, that it would take them to safety.[26] Down the road they encountered shattered remnants of Task Force Smith. Infantrymen, covered with the stinking mud of the rice paddies, seeing them, tottered onto the road. The convoy rescued about a hundred of them. Smith, wanting to collect as many men as he could, drove slowly down the path looking on either side for his troops. Miller Perry and a handful of others rushed ahead, to get word to headquarters. They raced toward Pyongtaek, hoping the tanks had not reached there first.

General Dean was at Taejon, and he was worried. He

wondered what was going on at Osan. His only contact with Task Force Smith was through Lieutenant Colonel Red Ayers at Pyongtaek, and the colonel told him communications with the advance force were out. For a while Dean waited anxiously, but his short supply of patience gave out. With a young aide he drove all afternoon and reached Ayers' headquarters after dark. Barth, who was still there, told him what little they knew, including the fact that tanks had been spotted well south of Osan. Task Force Smith was obviously overrun, perhaps even wiped out. Dean stalled a while but had to return to headquarters. He left just before Colonel Perry arrived. [27]

Marguerite Higgins was at Pyongtaek waiting in Red Ayers' hut for word from Osan. About one in the morning she was lying restlessly on the floor when another correspondent, Carl Mydans, came and whispered to her: "Better get into the war room fast." Higgins describes the scene there: "A kerosene light flaring on the table in front of them highlighted their serious faces. . . . Separating the officers from the relentless downpour outside were grotesque rain-soaked blankets that slapped over the windows. . . . Near us various officers were frantically grinding their field telephones which cast strange shadows in the melodramatic light." Barth and Ayers stood in the middle of the room leaning over a table covered with maps and field telephones. Three ragged soldiers, relics of Smith's unit, were leaving, one limping badly. They had just briefed Barth and Ayers about the skirmish at Osan, and their story was not encouraging. [28]

Perry arrived a few minutes later, the blood from his leg wound a dark stain on his pants. He was in agony, exhausted, and was having difficulty walking. "I'm sorry, sir," he told Barth. "We couldn't stop them." He reported how most of the tanks had driven straight through the artillery's curtain of fire and how the North Korean infantry had outflanked them. He spoke with slow military precision. He said that they had been outnumbered, that they had run out of ammunition, and that they had been forced to leave the litter cases. It was bad, he said. Barth, an experienced soldier, could visualize what had happened and the picture was dreadful. He also recognized the immediate implications: The enemy would be at Pyongtaek soon. "My God," he groaned, "to think I personally pulled away the dynamite from those bridges." Then, no doubt suddenly aware of the listening journalists, Barth said with false enthusiasm—like the coach of an outclassed football team, behind by four touchdowns at halftime—"You did a magnificent job. . . . You got seven tanks and we'll keep whittling them down."[29]

American losses were not high by the standards of most modern wars. Of the original 540 soldiers dug into the hills above Osan about 380 to 400 came back. (The number of casualties at Osan is hard to determine. Military reports during the next few weeks were confused. Incoming stragglers constantly altered estimates. Precise records were nonexistent.)

Seventy or so were captured; many of these died during the next eight months—of exposure, malnutrition, mistreatment, and simple humiliation. (Stories would be told of men in prison camps who gave up psychologically, partly because of their shame, sitting in corners amidst their own filth, their heads covered with blankets, until they died.) The rest of the missing men had been killed in action.[30]

The army now had some logistical problems. For one thing it had a number of corpses on its hands. On July 2 the Eighth Army's Quartermaster's office in Japan sent a note to headquarters that it had received twenty-three bodies from Korea (apparently most from the crash of a C-54). The quartermasters remarked that they did not have facilities for all these bodies, and they hoped, they said peevishly, that in the future some other arrangement could be made. Headquarters sent a liaison officer to Pusan to establish a cemetery there, "before," an army report stated, "the situation got out of hand." Graves Registration was now at work. It would be busy.[31]

Osan's wounded also created a problem. An hour after Perry reported to General Barth, casualties began to arrive at Pyongtaek, loaded on a railroad car. Most were sent to Japan. (They were lucky; wounded South Koreans went to an overcrowded, much less hygienic hospital in Taejon.) Within a few days the Eighth Army set up a hospital in Pusan and attached a M.A.S.H. unit to the Twenty-fourth Division.[32]

(Back in Japan the first casualty reports arrived at Camp Wood: five men missing in action. Their women and children cried. An ancient ritual of all wars was thus fulfilled.)

The first fatality reported back in the United States was perhaps symptomatic of the entire war. It was a stupid, purposeless death, inaccurately reported. It occurred south of Osan some hours after the battle. Several correspondents at Pyongtaek had heard about the breakthrough of North Korean tanks and had joined some American soldiers sent up the road to look for them. Among the enlisted men was Private Kenneth Shadrick, a nineteen-year-old boy from Skin Fork, West Virginia. It was his job to hold a bazooka on his shoulder and aim it at tanks not far away. It was a very dangerous task but he had already done it successfully a couple of times when the reporters arrived. He died because a press photographer wanted a better picture of him shooting his bazooka. Shadrick, a hillbilly, a high school dropout, agreed to do his best for History and Journalistic Realism. He raised up with his bazooka and started to point it at a North Korean tank. The tank's machine gun shot him in the chest. Shadrick tumbled soundlessly into the mud.

Later a passing medic looked at him and shook his head. "What a place to die," he muttered.[33]

Osan was the war's first battle. In a real sense it was Lexington, it was Pearl Harbor, it was Bull Run.

Pentagon officials called it a "classical tactical maneuver," but this was nonsense. Osan was the stuff of war: confused, bloody, marked by occasional heroism, but totally without grandeur. War has no romance—journalists and historians provide it with its false glamor. They come to the battleground afterward, pushing corpses to and fro, pressing them into acceptable, heroic positions, rubbing traces of rouge on chalky cheeks to make the deaths less ugly than they were, then return to their typewriters to give war a panache it does not deserve.

CHAPTER THIRTEEN

An
End to
Beginnings

Butterfly days slipped away,
    and Summer shrugged the grains of sand from her shoulders,
    gathered up the last remnants of the picnic—
        gum wrappers and brown bags,
        half-chewed franks and wrinkled damp towels,
        tin pails,
        shells,
        a frayed lawn chair—
and squinting into the setting sun,
        trudged,
            trailing memories
                into September.

IN A WAY OSAN was a victory for the Democratic People's Republic. The North Koreans only lost about half as many men in the battle as the United States.[1]

Did Americans who died in the skirmish, therefore, die for nothing? Was the sacrifice worth it, even in cold-war currency of "prestige," of "face"?

Osan accomplished several things—for good or ill. First, it proved the war would not be over soon. North Korean soldiers were not going to flee in panic at the sight of American military might. This fact destroyed most of America's Pollyanna-ish optimism, and Truman's government immediately began to prepare for a new military situation. On July 7 Charlie Ross, the president's press secretary, handed out a news release announcing that the United States was expanding its armed forces. [2]

Osan was not a complete debacle. When Task Force Smith went up Route 1 to meet the enemy, its primary purpose, realistically, had only been to stall the North Korean advance. In this, the GIs may have succeeded. Although the North Korean army continued to move south after Osan, it slowed down. "The enemy commander," MacArthur later wrote, "at once brought his advance to a stop to permit the laborious bringing up of artillery from across the [Han] river." According to MacArthur the American army had gained ten days. [3] These ten days allowed the United States to pour men and materiel into Pusan and prevented the imminent collapse of South Korea.

But Osan revealed a serious flaw in the American soldier. He was often brave, he was occasionally admirable, he was sometimes vicious, but he was not a well-disciplined *fighter*.

About a month after Osan three high-ranking officers, including Matthew Ridgway, met in Washington to discuss the combat effectiveness of the American army. Their conversation was not optimistic. As the secret memorandum of their meeting noted, they thought "The quality of the soldier now engaged in Korea is not up to World War II standards." Not only did the average soldier there lack infantry training and fail to camouflage himself when he should have, he was fuzzy on artillery details and weak on communications. Most of all, the memorandum reiterated again and again, he lacked combat courage. (In army terminology, he displayed an "absence of an aggressive fighting spirit.") At times in the war's first few weeks, the memorandum continued, some troops easily stampeded. "When attacked they do not respond with the fundamental infantry reaction of fire and movement, but instead call for artillery and air support and then withdraw if this does not suffice to interrupt the attack."[4]

American troops preferred obliterating an enemy, laying down a massive artillery barrage or air bombardment, to attacking him with foot soldiers. This tendency, while preserving *American* lives, led to increasing destructiveness and an almost complete lack of concern for (enemy) human life. To save Americans in some kind of "clean" way ("surgical" is another euphemistic word), to avoid the face-to-face confrontation with the consequences of one's acts, to fly amid blue sky and fleecy clouds to drop bombs on unseen ground far below, to take a leading part in the growing slaughter of the twentieth century—these became part of the American Way. Not only was this trend more inhumane, it also led to an emotional dependence on heavy weaponry—and the concomitant result was that it reduced the effectiveness of the foot soldier.

Osan also revealed that road-bound Americans stuck too closely to their trucks and jeeps, to their vehicular crutches. The North Koreans (and later the Chinese, and even later the North Vietnamese) proved better open-field fighters than most American GIs.

Osan provided an indication of another, deeply malignant, problem that would become more evident as the fighting went on. John Osborne, a senior correspondent for *Life* and *Time,* wrote from Korea that the war was brutalizing American troops. Fought the way the United States was doing it, it was beginning to "force upon our men in the field acts and attitudes of the utmost savagery. This means not the usual inevitable savagery of combat in the field, but savagery in detail—the blotting out of villages where the enemy *might* be hiding; the shooting and shelling of refugees who may include North Koreans."

American troops, Osborne continued, were becoming terrified by stories of North Koreans masquerading as refugees, who suddenly would pull machine guns or hand grenades from apparently harmless piles of household belongings and turn them on unsuspecting GIs. North and South Koreans were impossible to tell apart; they had the same stature, wore the same clothing, cut their hair the same. Osborne described an incident symptomatic of the brutalizing fear and confusion American soldiers felt when they had to fight in Asia. Several hundred Korean refugees were stumbling along a dirt road leading past an American regiment. When the regimental colonel discovered the refugees were coming, he said, "Don't let them through. But try to talk to them, try to tell them to go back."

"Yeah," said someone, "but what if they don't go back?"

"Well, then," the colonel slowly replied, "fire over their heads."

"O.K.," another officer said, "we fire over their heads. Then what?"

"Well, then," sighed the colonel, "fire into them if you have to. *If you have to,* I said."

Suspicion and tension. The kind of fear felt by the rich kid up the block forced to walk through the poor side of town. Or by whites in a car finding themselves lost on a ghetto side-street. As Osborne wrote, "Here is none of the camaraderie of G.I. and child everywhere else that the U.S. army has gone."[5] (Douglas MacArthur ordered the Eighth Army in Japan to distribute Osborne's article as widely as possible.)

In a war involving two different cultures, neither side feels akin to the other. Every time American soldiers have faced people who are completely different, they have tended to be brutal. George Washington fought the British with greater humanity than he did the Iroquois. During the Civil War blue-coated cavalry showed less brutality toward Southerners than they did a few years later toward Indians on the western plains.

In September 1950 David Shelby, thirteen years old, went to the Oregon State Fair, where he turned in his 4-H Club "record book." Its total entries for the months of June and July went like this:

> June: Blossom had a calf, and I haven't decided what to name it.
> I exhibited at the spring Jersey show and didn't do too well.
> July: Nothing special happened, except our house burned down.

To David Shelby the birth of Blossom's calf was the only notable event that summer. Everything else, even the fire which destroyed his home, paled into insignificance.

David Shelby was wrong. Although he apparently was unaware of war in faraway Korea, something "special" had indeed happened. Even though each person's life has its own private rhythms, and even though these often seem unconnected to outside events, the decisions of an American president alter the world almost as inexorably as an ice age. Harry S. Truman had led his country into war, and the echoes would not die for a long time.

The following are some of the results of these two weeks in the summer of 1950.

The retreat from Osan and the others that followed pushed the Americans south toward Pusan. It almost seemed as if they might lose this war, but as they were squeezed into a smaller and smaller knot in the southeast tip of Korea, they became like a contracted muscle. As their lines became less confused and amorphous, as they dug in near Pusan, they could face the North Koreans in a traditionally Western, linear war. After they had rooted their flanks firmly on both sides, the Inmun Gun was directly in front of them. Now, at last, United States airpower became fully effective. (As battle lines become clear and rigid, strafing and bombing become devastating weapons.) By early September—ten weeks after it had begun—the war had been resolved. It would only be a matter of time.

Then Douglas MacArthur decided to accelerate the process with a dramatic (and risky) amphibious invasion at Inchon, far behind North Korean lines. It worked: Caught in a pincers, the Inmun Gun snapped back and scattered, followed hotly by the victorious American and South Korean armies. By late in September the "bandits" had fled the scene of the crime. The "police action" was complete.

For reasons which are still not entirely clear, MacArthur and the American government chose to cross the Thirty-eighth Parallel, to eliminate the Pyongyang government entirely, and to put the two pieces of Korea together again. The purpose of the military venture thus changed from *evicting* the North Korean intruders to *destroying* them. This new character of the war, however, was dangerous. Mao's government had indicated quite clearly throughout late September that if the United States crossed the Parallel, China would enter the war. But Truman and MacArthur downplayed the threat.

When the American army drew close to the Yalu River, which separated North Korea from northeast China, completing the last mop-up of the Inmun Gun, 300,000 Chinese troops attacked. Suddenly a small, almost colonial, war became much bigger.

In the following weeks the United States army retreated, the longest withdrawal in its history. In Japan MacArthur became at once enraged and depressed. In November he had confidently announced that his troops would be home by Christmas. Now he faced total—and *personal*—humiliation. (Generals who allow their armies to become surrounded and ambushed are seldom honored. Their mistakes are studied—and *ridiculed*—in military textbooks.) MacArthur had erred, badly. But a man of his temperament could not have admitted it; his psyche could not have accepted the responsibility. He had to find a scapegoat for his calamitous blunders, and he struck out in all directions, particularly against his commander-in-chief. He concluded that Truman

—this petty little undistinguished man—was muddled in his conceptions about this war. "There is no substitute for victory," the general in Tokyo kept insisting. We should take the war directly against China, he said, and not fight a mere holding action, a limited war, in Korea.

Truman disagreed. He never lost sight of his main focus, Europe. To become more deeply involved in Asia was not only flirting with a vast world conflagration, it made the United States less effective in Europe.

Given their personalities—each abrasive to the other—and their contradictory goals, conflict between these two men was almost inevitable. In the spring of 1951, with the unanimous agreement of the Joint Chiefs, Truman fired MacArthur.

The general returned to a hero's welcome, though his popularity seemed based more on frustration over an extended limited war than on any love for MacArthur himself. Soon, in fact, the cheering died and the old soldier faded away.

The war stumbled on for the next two years without "victory." It settled into a grim, bloody stalemate near the original Parallel. It took another president, Eisenhower, to bring it to an unsatisfying close in 1953.

As far as the Korean nation itself was concerned, what were the results of those two weeks in 1950?

Syngman Rhee's regime, which had been in serious political trouble in May 1950, was solidified by the war and American intervention. Rhee eventually fell in 1960 and his place was taken by a military government. Since then, South Korea has become reasonably prosperous, especially for her well-to-do classes, and though she is hardly an open, democratic society, she offers, compared to most Asian countries, a certain degree of "freedom."

The war itself, of course, decimated Korea, the very nation the United States was theoretically attempting to save. Precise calculations are impossible, but clearly the number of Koreans *killed* runs into the millions, and upward to 10 million more were homeless. Factories were destroyed, farmland was ruined, railroads were ripped up. To save Korea.

If Truman had not decided to enter the conflict, North Korea would certainly have conquered the South and unified the country. In retrospect it might be asked, Would this eventuality have been an unmitigated calamity for Korea? Would it have been worse than what did happen? It is true that since the war ended, the North Korean regime of Kim Il Sung has been one of the most repressive governments in the world, but on the other hand it does face a hostile opponent to the south, supported by a large foreign (American) military contingent. One can argue that if North Korea had won easily in 1950, the victory might have mellowed it, especially if the United States had been willing to offer it a tiny fraction of the billions of dollars she has since spent to buttress the Republic of Korea.

The summer of 1950 also had major effects on Asia as a whole. The United States became identified, and identified itself, as the anti-Communist bastion for the entire continent. No longer was America propping up only the governments of Western Europe; she had taken a stand throughout Asia: in Korea, in Indochina, in Japan, in the Philippines. The implications were clear: America would pay any price, bear any burden, meet any hardship, support any friend, oppose any foe to assure the survival and the success of "un-Communism."

Ironically, Truman's decisions probably helped Mao Tse-tung strengthen his own position in China. For the next two decades Mao was able to use the United States as a bogeyman, to force unification upon his country.

Did the United States gain "face" in Asia by entering the war? There is of course no way of judging these things, but the answer may be found in the following story.

Early in the war two reporters happened upon a toothless

hag living in a hut. An ROK flag hung prominently near the
door. After the two Americans talked to her for a moment,
she slyly showed them her other, North Korean, flag, which
she was keeping in case she ever needed it.

"Whose side are you on?" one of the reporters kidded her.

She cackled and replied, "I'm on your side. You have the
most guns."[6]

In the United States Acheson and Truman used the war
to get congressional approval for, among other things, an
armed NATO and an accelerated and expensive H-bomb
project. The National Security Council's secret plan of the
previous winter, NSC-68, went into effect almost immediately. Since the government had wanted to move in this
direction anyway, early losses—like Osan—played right into
its hands. Truman and his advisers had not conspiratorially
planned this, but they were an opportunistic crew and they
took advantage of such apparent military disasters.

There were other effects. The American presidency, as
an institution, swelled with pride and power. Henceforth,
emissaries from afar brought tribute to it. Runners came in
gasping Secrets. ("The Russians are ahead.... The Russians are behind.... The Croatians are plotting against the
Montenegrins.") Only the president knew for sure. A
monopoly over such arcane bits of knowledge can give one a
delicious sense of Power. (Threads of a singsong ten-year-
old's voice: "I-know-something-you-don't-know.")

The presidency had also expanded its authority over foreign affairs. Presidents could apparently now decide matters
of peace and war without consulting anyone beyond a few
chosen advisers.

As for Truman himself, his popularity soared—briefly.
Seventy-seven percent of those polled approved of his initial
moves in Korea.[7] Harry S. Truman, the unpretentious,

decent, democratic, shrewd hack politician from Independence, Missouri, the flag-bearer in this jihad, had become "the tough little guy who couldn't be pushed around," the James Cagney of international politics. But as the war dragged on through the autumn and into the next year, support for it—and him—dropped off.[8] (His popularity would not return until long after he left office, when he began to grow into a legendary and heroic Everyman.)

In the elections that fall, Republicans won a number of new places all across the country. In California, for instance, Richard Nixon defeated Helen Gahagan Douglas for a seat in the Senate. Earlier, when he had announced his candidacy, this young, curly-headed congressman said that "The issue . . . is the choice between freedom and socialist baloney. They can call it planned economy, the Fair Deal, or social welfare. It's still the same old socialist baloney any way you slice it."[9] Douglas herself later blamed the Korean War for her defeat, but the real reason probably lay in more prosaic matters like inflation and a growing national boredom with the tired clichés Democratic politicians were inclined to use. The war *may* have had some effect on the November elections, but, if so, any such impact is probably impossible to measure precisely.

On the other hand, it is clear that while the Korean War did not create the anti-Communist spasm called "McCarthyism," it did encourage greater—vigilance. The war, at least the way Truman presented it, seemed a struggle against communism, and it therefore made the vague specter of The Red Menace much more palpable, and thus added great impetus to anti-radicalism in the United States. Within a few weeks after it began, the city fathers of Laurel, Mississippi, passed a resolution making it illegal for a Communist to enter their town, and patriotic citizens in Chicago stoned a Communist bookstore. During the same period the American Medical Association launched a campaign against "the danger of socialized medicine," in order, it said, to protect America "on the civilian front." In September the Monogram movie company dropped plans to film Longfellow's *Hiawatha;* the story line, it claimed, was too leftist.

Joe McCarthy became the most famous proponent of this phenomenon. Senator Millard Tydings of Maryland had chaired the committee designed to squelch McCarthy's original charges that summer, and when Tydings lost his reelection campaign (almost entirely over local issues), a great myth was born. Many people believed, mistakenly, that the senator from Wisconsin had immense political clout. McCarthy himself was willing to ride the crest of this belief. For a while it seemed as if he was blamed—or praised—for everything. James Thurber, who should have known better, said that because of Joe McCarthy "humor fell off at the *New Yorker* and throughout the nation."[10] The facts were that Thurber and all those who thought McCarthy had "gotten" Tydings were wrong. McCarthy had no broad political base of his own. He was the Wizard of Oz. He was important only as long as newspapermen and politicians feared him. Eventually, when they tentatively challenged him, his power suddenly vanished. He became merely a sad figure with rumpled clothes and red-rimmed eyes, wafting the odor of whiskey, staggering forlornly and alone through the corridors of the Senate.

And so the string was played out, the effects of the summer of 1950 drifted away into the future. McCarthy, inflation, Mao, the November elections, the Huks, MacArthur—the good days and the bad.

The men at Blair House during the warm days of late June had assumed that the war would be a quick one, almost a mere show of strength. They foresaw few of the consequences of their decisions. One wonders, therefore, if they had a chance to do it all over again, would they have done the same?

Some years later someone pointed out to Dean Acheson that maybe if they had known what the Korean War was going to involve, they would have avoided it.

Acheson replied with a smile, "Isn't that also true of the procreation of the race?"[11]

Perhaps.

Notes

CHAPTER ONE

1. Harry Vaughan Oral History, Truman Library.
2. J. B. West, *Upstairs at the White House*, pp. 76–77.
3. Merle Miller, speech-interview, May 17, 1975; Jonathan Daniels, *The Man of Independence*, p. 70.
4. Miller, speech-interview.
5. Letter to the author, name withheld by request.
6. Frederick Lewis Allen, *The Big Change*, pp. 191–92.
7. Kenneth R. Young, interview, October 6, 1975.
8. *New York Herald Tribune*, July 8, 1950, p. 16.
9. *New York Times*, June 28, 1950, p. 25.
10. *Ibid.*, July 4, 1950, p. 1.
11. Julian Symons, *Crime*, p. 226.
12. *Time*, May 15, 1950, p. 38.
13. *Ibid.*, May 1, 1950, p. 86.
14. *Public Opinion Quarterly*, XIV (Spring 1950), 180, 187, 189, 192; (Fall 1950), 594, 599.
15. *Ibid.* (Spring 1950), 182; (Fall 1950), 602.
16. *Ibid.* (Fall 1950), 609.
17. *Time*, November 13, 1950, p. 85; May 1, 1950, p. 34; March 20, 1950, p. 77.

CHAPTER TWO

1. Walt Sheldon, *The Honorable Conquerors*, p. 46.
2. O. H. P. King, *Tail of the Paper Tiger*, p. 188.

3. George Sam, interview, March 8, 1974.

4. *New York Times,* June 22, 1950, p. 5.

5. Keyes Beech, *Tokyo and Points East,* p. 145.

6. Eighth Army, G-1, "Prologue, G-1 Activity," Box "Army 5," Truman Library.

7. J. Lawton Collins, *War in Peacetime,* p. 67.

8. Interview, source withheld by request.

9. Sheldon, *Honorable Conquerors,* p. 115.

CHAPTER THREE

1. James F. Schnabel, *Policy and Direction: The First Year, The United States Army in the Korean War,* pp. 8–11; J. Lawton Collins, *War in Peacetime,* pp. 25–26n; Dean Rusk, letter to the author, September 10, 1973.

2. ATIS Interrogation Report No. 1417, Field Report (ADVATIS— 0887), MacArthur Library. Kim was captured near Pusan, South Korea, on September 20, 1973.

3. The best books on the Democratic People's Republic are Robert A. Scalapino and Chong-sik Lee, *Communism in Korea;* Koon Woo Nam, *The North Korean Communist Leadership, 1945–1965;* Dae-sook Suh, *The Korean Communist Movement, 1918–1948;* Robert R. Simmons, *The Strained Alliance: Peking, P'yongyang, Moscow and the Korean War;* and Joyce and Gabriel Kolko, *The Limits of Power,* pp. 276–99.

4. Simmons, *Strained Alliance,* pp. 22–25.

5. See Baik Bong, *Kim Il Sung.* This is the only extended biography, but it is so fawningly hagiological it is laughable. Perhaps the best biography is Chong-sik Lee, "Kim Il-song of North Korea," *Asian Survey,* VII (June 1967), 374–82.

6. Robert T. Oliver, *Syngman Rhee: The Man Behind the Myth,* is an authorized and highly flattering biography; Richard C. Allen, *Korea's Syngman Rhee: An Unauthorized Portrait,* is more objective.

7. Memorandum, R. D. Muir to Matt Connelly, February 24, 1947, Official File, Truman Library.

8. See, for example, George M. McCune, *Korea Today, passim.*

9. *The Economist,* July 1, 1950, p. 23; *New York Times,* January 25, 1950, p. 5; American Military Government, National Economics Board,

South Korean Interim Government Activities, XXXXIV (July-August 1948), 213; *New York Times,* September 6, 1949, p. 9, and February 1, 1950, p. 9; Kolko and Kolko, *Limits of Power,* p. 569; Harold Joyce Noble, *Embassy at War,* p. 255.

10. Simmons, *Strained Alliance,* p. 104; Simmons, "The Korean Civil War," in *Without Parallel,* p. 146.

11. ATIS 315, July 21, 1950.

12. See, for example, Kolko and Kolko, *Limits of Power,* p. 567; William Dean and William L. Worden, *General Dean's Story,* p. 64.

13. *New York Times,* June 26, 1950, p. 2; June 28, 1950, p. 18.

14. While there are many defenders of this theory, three are representative: I. F. Stone, *The Hidden History of the Korean War;* Karunaker Gupta, "How Did the Korean War Begin?" in *China Quarterly* (October-December 1972), pp. 699–716; Alan N. Kopke, "The Beginnings of the Korean War" (unpublished manuscript, n.d.). I would like to thank Gabriel Kolko for loaning me his copy of Kopke's paper.

15. George V. Allen, Oral Interview, John Foster Dulles MSS, Princeton University Library, p. 23.

16. Perhaps another reason tanks were withheld was that General William L. Roberts, in charge of the American advisers, insisted that tanks would be of no military value in the soggy paddies of Korea. See Robert K. Sawyer, *Military Advisers in Korea: KMAG in Peace and War,* pp. 100–01. For Roberts' opinion, see Noble, *Embassy at War,* p. 226.

17. Noble, *Embassy at War,* p. 230. On the apparently fictitious attack on Haeju, see *ibid.,* pp. 267–68.

18. Kolko and Kolko, *Limits of Power,* Chapter 21; Simmons, *Strained Alliance,* pp. 22–38, 102–36; Simmons, "Korean Civil War."

CHAPTER FOUR

1. No major biography of Muccio exists. *Who's Who* and the various Foreign Service lists carry brief outlines; see, also, Harold Joyce Noble, *Embassy at War, passim.*

2. *New York Times,* June 27, 1950, p. 6; John C. Caldwell, *The Korea Story,* p. 95. Caldwell's book, while biased from a highly conservative, evangelical point of view, is an excellent and devastating depiction of ugly Americans overseas. See, especially, pp. 73–80.

3. Keyes Beech, *Tokyo and Points East*, p. 133.

4. Quoted in Robert K. Sawyer, *Military Advisers in Korea: KMAG in Peace and War*, p. 43.

5. *Ibid.*, p. 44.

6. *The Statesman's Year-Book, 1950*, p. 1186. The number of Catholic churches is obscure since so many of them were attached to European—for example, Belgian—missions which did not fall under AMIK.

7. *New York Times*, July 5, 1950, p. 2.

8. William R. Mathews, *With Dulles in Korea and Japan*, p. 5; Noble, *Embassy at War*, p. 222.

9. Caldwell, *Korea Story*, p. 163; Noble, *Embassy at War*, p. 15.

10. Caldwell, *Korea Story*, pp. 163–65.

11. A. Kristian Jensen, *Internment, North Korea*; T. A. Brumbaugh, *My Marks and Scars I Carry*.

12. *Editor and Publisher*, July 22, 1950, p. 10.

13. For the early hours of the war, see Sawyer, *Military Advisers in Korea*, pp. 114–19; Roy E. Appleman, *South to the Naktong, North to the Yalu*, pp. 19–30.

14. *New York Times*, June 30, 1950, p. 2.

15. Sawyer, *Military Advisers in Korea*, p. 118. Beech, *Tokyo and Points East*, p. 11, mentions that Major Walter Greenwood, at that moment head of KMAG, first received word at 5:30. For the story of the next few hours, see *Editor and Publisher*, July 22, 1950, p. 10; Glenn D. Paige, *The Korean Decision*, pp. 82–84, 88; Noble, *Embassy at War*, pp. 12–14, 241–42; O. H. P. King, *Tail of the Paper Tiger*, p. 104.

16. Department of State, *United States Policy in the Korean Crisis*, p. 1.

17. Caldwell, *Korea Story*, p. 166.

18. *New York Times*, June 25, 1950, p. 2.

19. *Ibid.*, June 26, 1950, p. 2.

20. Caldwell, *Korea Story*, p. 168.

21. Quoted in Paige, *Korean Decision*, p. 105.

22. Appleman, *South to the Naktong*, p. 29, puts the blame solely on Chae. Frank Baldwin, editor of Noble's *Embassy at War*, suggests that Defense Minister Sihn Sung Mo helped formulate the plan, and furthermore that both Sihn and Chae were pushed into such a patently ridiculous plan by high-ranking members of the government, including Rhee (p. 246). Baldwin, whose editing job on Noble's diary is a superb example of how editing should be done, seems to be in error on this

matter. He states that the meeting which drew up this plan occurred on June 26. Actually, the order went out the previous day and therefore could not have resulted from any such meeting. Either the meeting was earlier or Chae alone was responsible.

CHAPTER FIVE

1. By far the best chronicle of the next twenty-four hours is Glenn D. Paige, *The Korean Decision,* pp. 88–143. Paige's account, based partly on numerous interviews with the participants, can be called semiofficial. See also a two-page "Chronology of Developments Following Communist Attack on the Republic of Korea, June 24–27, 1950" (based on "Special Collection," Historical Division, Department of State; Albert L. Warner, "How the Korea Decision Was Made," *Harper's,* June 1951, p. 99. The manuscript division of the Truman Library contains fascinating documents among the George Elsey papers. Shortly after these events Truman asked Elsey, a young assistant at the White House who had majored in history at college, to draw up a file of information of these days. In the file is a copy of Warner's article with Elsey's handwritten criticisms in the margins. Elsey, rightly, did not think much of it.

2. David Halberstam, *The Best and the Brightest,* pp. 324–25.

3. See a "Chronology of Events" among the Bradley papers at West Point.

4. U.S. Congress, Senate, Armed Services Committee and Foreign Relations Committee, *Military Situation in the Far East,* 82d Cong., 1st sess., 1951, p. 2572.

5. Merle Miller, *Plain Speaking,* p. 269; Dean Acheson, *Present at the Creation,* p. 402; *Time,* March 6, 1950, p. 41.

6. There is a discrepancy between Acheson's memoirs on the next few hours and the recollections of the other participants. Acheson, *Present at the Creation,* p. 402; Miller, *Plain Speaking,* pp. 269–70; "Princeton Seminars," p. 14, Dean Acheson MSS, Truman Library. Paige's account, in *Korean Decision,* pp. 91–92, seems somewhat more plausible.

7. *New York Times,* June 29, 1950, p. 12.

8. Miller, *Plain Speaking,* p. 267n.

9. George Elsey MSS; Acheson, *Present at the Creation,* p. 405; Miller, *Plain Speaking,* p. 270.

10. *New York Times,* June 26, 1950, p. 9.

11. John M. Chang, Oral Interview, John Foster Dulles MSS, Princeton University Library; *Washington Star,* June 25, 1950, p. 1.

12. For the following section on the UN, see Paige, *Korean Decision,* pp. 95–96; State Department "Chronology of Developments," p. 2; Miller, *Plain Speaking,* pp. 270–72; Trygve Lie, *In the Cause of Peace,* p. 327; Warner, "How the Korea Decision Was Made," p. 100. The recollections of each participant vary slightly.

13. U.S. Department of State, *United States Policy in the Korean Crisis,* p. 15.

14. Matthew B. Ridgway, *The Korean War,* p. 24.

15. J. Lawton Collins, *War in Peacetime,* pp. 1–2.

16. *New York Herald Tribune,* June 26, 1950, p. 2.

17. *New York Times,* June 26, 1950, p. 7.

18. Miller, *Plain Speaking,* p. 273.

19. *New York Times,* June 26, 1950, p. 7.

20. *Ibid.*

21. *Ibid.,* July 2, 1950, Section IV, p. 1.

22. Margaret Truman, *Souvenir,* p. 275. Emphasis added.

CHAPTER SIX

1. Alonzo Fields, *My 21 Years in the White House,* p. 100.

2. Beverly Smith, "Why We Went to War in Korea," *Saturday Evening Post,* November 10, 1951, p. 76.

3. *Time,* April 30, 1950, p. 23.

4. Dean Acheson, *Present at the Creation,* p. 405.

5. Harry S. Truman, *Memoirs.* Vol. 2, *Years of Trial and Hope,* p. 379.

6. Memorandum, June 26, 1950, George Elsey MSS, Truman Library.

7. See, for example, Ronald J. Caridi, *The Korean War and American Politics,* p. 29.

8. Acheson, *Present at the Creation,* p. 407.

9. J. Lawton Collins, *War in Peacetime,* pp. 29–30.

10. U.S. Senate, Foreign Relations Committee, *Economic Assistance to China and Korea: Hearings,* 81st Cong., 1st–2d sess., 1949–1950 (released 1974), pp. 179–80.

11. Quoted in James F. Schnabel, *Policy and Direction: The First Year, The United States Army in the Korean War,* p. 33.

12. See, for example, Ernest R. May, *"Lessons" of the Past,* pp. 54–55.

13. *Time*, August 14, 1950, p. 8; August 7, 1950, p. 17; *New York Times*, June 22, 1950, p. 21.

14. Philip C. Jessup, *The Birth of Nations*, pp. 25, 26, 29.

15. U.S. Department of State, "Memorandum of Conversation," June 25, 1950, hereafter referred to as BHC #1. These are the notes of that evening's Blair House conference, dictated almost immediately afterward by Philip Jessup.

16. *Public Opinion Quarterly*, XIV (Winter 1950–1951), 815.

17. On the position of the Republican party toward China, see Bradford H. Westerfield, *Foreign Policy and Party Politics*, pp. 241–44.

18. *New York Times*, June 24, 1950, p. 4; June 26, 1950, p. 14.

19. Beyond the revelations to congressional committees in 1976, dozens of works touch on this subject. The best short analysis is Schnabel, *Policy and Direction*, pp. 61–65.

20. See teleconference minutes between the Pentagon and Tokyo, June 25, 1950, Elsey MSS.

21. *Ibid.*, July 2, 1950, Section IV, p. 1.

22. See BHC #1.

23. "Princeton Seminars," p. 14, Dean Acheson MSS, Truman Library.

24. Smith, "Why We Went to War," p. 76.

25. "Princeton Seminars," p. 9.

26. Glenn D. Paige, *The Korean Decision*, p. 126.

27. BHC #1 for most of the following.

28. Charles E. Bohlen, *Witness to History, 1929–1969*, p. 292.

29. "Princeton Seminars," p. 11.

30. *Ibid.*, p. 12.

31. Paige, *Korean Decision*, p. 141. Webb's apparently inappropriate suggestion or his earlier abstruse remark may be the reason he was the only member of that night's group not to take part in the next meeting.

32. "Teleconference, 252330Z," Elsey MSS.

CHAPTER SEVEN

1. Glenn D. Paige, *The Korean Decision*, pp. 86–87.

2. "Princeton Seminars," p. 10, Dean Acheson MSS, Truman Library.

3. William R. Mathews, *With Dulles in Korea and Japan*, p. 22.

4. John M. Allison, *Ambassador from the Prairie*, p. 128. Most of the

following section came from Allison, pp. 128–31, and from Allison's interview, pp. 10–12, Dulles Oral History, Princeton University Library. See, also William J. Sebald, *With MacArthur in Japan*, p. 183–85.

5. Mathews, *With Dulles*, pp. 17–20.

6. *New York Times*, June 26, 1950, p. 3.

7. William F. Dean, *General Dean's Story*, p. 14.

8. Allison, *Ambassador*, p. 132; Allison, interview, p. 11.

9. Much of the following is contained in Harold Joyce Noble, *Embassy at War*, pp. 21–26. See, also, Robert K. Sawyer, *Military Advisers in Korea: KMAG in Peace and War*, pp. 121–22; John C. Caldwell, *The Korea Story*, pp. 170–71; David Duncan, *Life*, July 10, 1950, p. 20.

10. Noble, *Embassy at War*, p. 23.

11. *Ibid.*, p. 25.

12. Eighth Army, G-4, "G-4 Unit History, 25 June to 30 June 1950," p. 2., Box "Army 5," Truman Library.

13. Caldwell, *Korea Story*, pp. 170–71.

14. Paige, *Korean Decision*, pp. 156–59; Dean Acheson, *Present at the Creation*, p. 407; "Memorandum of Conversation," with John Myun Chang, George Elsey MSS, Truman Library; "Conversation, Truman and Elsey," Elsey MSS; Dr. John Myun Chang, Oral Interview, Dulles Oral History, Princeton Library; *New York Times*, June 27, 1950, p. 4.

15. Paige, *Korean Decision*, p. 161; Acheson, *Present at the Creation*, p. 407.

16. Beverly Smith, "Why We Went to War in Korea," *Saturday Evening Post*, November 10, 1951, p. 80.

17. U.S. Department of State, "Memorandum of Conversation," June 26, 1950.

18. Sebald, *With MacArthur*, p. 186; Allison, *Ambassador*, pp. 136–38.

19. U.S. Congress, Senate, Armed Services Committee and Foreign Relations Committee, *Military Situation in the Far East*, 82d Cong., 1st sess., 1951, p. 231.

20. "Teleconference with MacArthur, 270217Z," June 26, 1950, Elsey MSS. Paige, *Korean Decision*, pp. 184–85, states MacArthur insisted Koreans be told of the decision, that they needed something to boost their morale, and that the Joint Chiefs okayed MacArthur's request—as long as the announcement only be made in Korea, so that no American find out about it before Truman's formal announcement about eight hours away. Paige's story is questionable, for almost no one—including

Koreans—recalled the broadcast. Syngman Rhee himself apparently only learned of Truman's decision many hours later, according to Noble, *Embassy at War*, pp. 73–74.

21. Roy E. Appleman, *South to the Naktong, North to the Yalu*, p. 40. For slightly different versions of this message, see Sawyer, *Military Advisers*, p. 125; and Marguerite Higgins, *War in Korea*, p. 20.

22. "Minutes," June 27, 1950, Elsey MSS; Acheson, *Present at the Creation*, p. 409; Smith, "Why We Went to War," p. 82.

23. "Princeton Seminars," p. 35. For a while that week, however, Acheson gave real thought to whether Truman should formally speak to Congress. "Memorandum," July 3, 1950, Elsey MSS.

24. U.S. Congress, Senate, 81st Cong., 2d sess., June 27, 1950, *Congressional Record*, XCVI, p. 9347.

25. "Memorandum," June 27, 1950, Elsey MSS.

26. *Congressional Record*, p. 9322.

27. *Chicago Tribune*, July 1, 1950, p. 4.

28. Lyndon Baines Johnson, *The Vantage Point*, p. 573.

29. *Congressional Record*, p. 9233.

30. *New York Times*, June 28, 1950, p. 4.

31. Vandenberg to Truman, July 3, 1950, Vandenberg MSS, William L. Clements Library, University of Michigan.

32. Allison, *Ambassador*, p. 139. For a general view of Republican reaction, see Ronald J. Caridi, "The G.O.P. and the Korean War," *Pacific Historical Review*, XXXVII (November 1968), 423–43; Caridi, *The Korean War and American Politics*.

33. *Christian Science Monitor*, June 29, 1950, p. 1.

34. *New York Times*, June 29, 1950, p. 5; Paige, p. 243.

35. "Minutes," June 27, 1950, Elsey MSS.

36. Paige, *Korean Decision*, pp. 200, 220.

37. Charles E. Bohlen, *Witness to History, 1929–1969*, p. 292.

38. Acheson, *Present at the Creation*, p. 411; "Princeton Seminars," p. 39.

CHAPTER EIGHT

1. Harold Joyce Noble, *Embassy at War*, pp. 30–32.
2. Walt Sheldon, *Hell or High Water*, p. 28.
3. Noble, *Embassy at War*, p. 62.

4. *New York Times,* June 29, 1950, p. 3; Keyes Beech, *Tokyo and Points East,* pp. 110–12.

5. Roy E. Appleman, *South to the Naktong, North to the Yalu,* pp. 32–33.

6. Marguerite Higgins, *War in Korea,* pp. 22–25; Appleman, *South to the Naktong,* p. 41.

7. *New York Times,* July 8, 1950, p. 2.

8. *Editor and Publisher,* July 1, 1950, p. 11; *New York Times,* June 29, 1950, p. 3; Beech, *Tokyo and Points East,* pp. 113–16.

9. Higgins, *War in Korea,* p. 25.

10. Appleman, *South to the Naktong,* pp. 33–34; Noble, *Embassy at War,* p. 263.

11. Robert K. Sawyer, *Military Advisers in Korea: KMAG in Peace and War,* p. 127; Appleman, *South to the Naktong,* p. 41; Higgins, *War in Korea,* pp. 26–30.

12. Appleman, *South to the Naktong,* pp. 43–44. Sheldon, *Hell or High Water,* who is much more imaginative than dependable, states (p. 29) that Tuesday night Muccio received word of MacArthur's arrival. If so, MacArthur's trip did not result from the collapse of Seoul or Church's reports but instead from MacArthur's itch to see what was happening for himself. Sheldon declares that his source for this information was Muccio, who may have been mistaken.

13. David Douglas Duncan, *This is War!,* p. 4.

14. *Newsweek,* July 10, 1950, p. 20.

15. Douglas MacArthur, *Reminiscences,* p. 332. He, of course, had smoked it in Japan on at least one previous occasion—see p. 107, Chapter Seven—but apparently not in public.

16. Appleman, *South to the Naktong,* p. 33; Glenn D. Paige, *The Korean Decision,* pp. 230–31.

17. Sheldon, *Hell or High Water,* p. 39; Noble, *Embassy at War,* p. 88.

18. Courtney Whitney, *MacArthur: His Rendezvous with Destiny,* p. 327.

19. Sheldon, *Hell or High Water,* p. 33.

20. Paige, *Korean Decision,* pp. 244–46, 230–31n.

21. This message is pieced together from Paige, *Korean Decision,* pp. 237–38, and James F. Schnabel, *Policy and Direction: The First Year, The United States Army in the Korean War,* pp. 77–78.

22. J. Lawton Collins, *War in Peacetime,* pp. 20–23, has the minutes from this conference.

23. Albert L. Warner, "How the Korea Decision Was Made," *Harper's,*
June 1951, p. 106.
24. Paige, *Korean Decision,* pp. 256–57.
25. *Ibid.,* pp. 257–60.
26. *Life,* July 10, 1950, pp. 30–31.

CHAPTER NINE

1. Roy E. Appleman, *South to the Naktong, North to the Yalu,* p. 60.
2. *New York Herald Tribune,* July 3, 1950, p. 1.
3. Colonel Philip S. Day, letter to author, May 3, 1973.
4. Colonel John Doody, letter to author, April 16, 1973.
5. Day, letter.
6. Diary, name withheld by request.
7. Appleman, *South to the Naktong,* p. 60.
8. *New York Times,* July 1, 1950, p. 1.
9. Appleman, *South to the Naktong,* p. 61.
10. U.S. Congress, Senate, Armed Services Committee and Foreign
Relations Committee, *Military Situation in the Far East,* 82d Cong., 1st
sess., 1951, p. 231.
11. The following section, unless specifically noted, comes from articles in the *New York Times,* the *New York Herald Tribune,* and the
Chicago Tribune.
12. Letter to the editor, *Chicago Tribune,* July 1, 1950, p. 8.
13. *Los Angeles Times,* July 9, 1950.
14. Charles P. Larrowe, *Harry Bridges,* p. 326.

CHAPTER TEN

1. The following, unless otherwise noted, comes from the *New York
Times,* the *New York Herald Tribune,* and the *Chicago Tribune.*
2. *New York Times,* July 5, 1950, p. 14.
3. "Note," June 30, 1950, George Elsey MSS, Truman Library;
"Princeton Seminars," p. 29, Dean Acheson MSS, Truman Library.
Truman's self-serving conversation with Merle Miller on this topic (see
Miller, *Plain Speaking,* pp. 282–83) is inaccurate.
4. Eighth Army, G-4, "G-4 Unit History, 1 July to 12 July, 1950," p. 1,
Box "Army 5," Truman Library.

5. O. H. P. King, *Tail of the Paper Tiger*, p. 191.

6. William F. Dean and William L. Worden, *General Dean's Story*, p. 5.

7. Fifty-second Field Artillery Battalion, "War Diary: July 1–July 12, 1950," National Archives.

8. "G-4 Unit History."

9. Keyes Beech, *Tokyo and Points East*, p. 7.

10. Roy E. Appleman, *South to the Naktong, North to the Yalu*, p. 65.

11. Twenty-first Regiment, "War Diary: July 1–July 31, 1950," National Archives.

12. *Chicago Tribune*, July 3, 1950, p. 1; W. Bartlett, ed., *With the Australians in Korea*, p. 174.

13. George B. Barth, "The First Days in Korea," *Army Combat Forces Journal*, II (March 1952), 21; Dean, *General's Story*, p. 20; Fifty-second Field Artillery Battalion, "War Diary." See also Appleman, *South to the Naktong*, p. 65, which is uncharacteristically mistaken about much of this day.

14. Fifty-second Field Artillery Battalion, "War Diary."

15. Twenty-first Regiment, "War Diary."

16. Barth "The First Days," p. 22; *St Louis Post-Dispatch*, July 6, 1950, p. 1.

17. *Chicago Tribune*, July 6, 1950, p. 4.

18. Miley to Ridgway, June 29, 1950. Matthew B. Ridgway MSS, Carlisle Barracks. Ridgway's approval is handwritten on Miley's letter.

19. U.S. Army Infantry School, *Characteristics of Infantry Weapons* (February 1966), p. 81.

20. *New York Herald Tribune*, July 5, 1950, p. 1; *New York Times*, July 6, 1950, pp. 2, 4; King, *Paper Tiger*, p. 181.

21. Al Mullikan, "The First Brutal Weeks in Korea," *Washington Post*, June 24, 1951.

CHAPTER ELEVEN

1. Al Mullikan, "The First Brutal Weeks in Korea," *Washington Post*, June 24, 1951.

2. Twenty-fourth Division, "War Diary: June 25 to July 7, 1950," National Archives.

3. ATIS Interrogation Report No. 1553, October 2, 1950, MacArthur Library.

4. Colonel Philip S. Day, letter to author, May 3, 1973.

5. *Ibid.*

6. *New York Times,* July 6, 1950, p. 3. See *New York Herald Tribune,* July 6, 1950, p. 3; George B. Barth, "The First Days in Korea," *Army Combat Forces Journal,* II (March 1952), 22.

7. Marguerite Higgins, *War in Korea,* p. 58.

8. Barth, "The First Days," p. 21; Higgins, *War in Korea,* pp. 58–59.

9. *New York Times,* July 6, 1950, p. 3.

10. Russell A. Gugeler, *Combat Actions in Korea,* pp. 6–7.

11. *New York Times,* July 5, 1950, p. 11.

12. Higgins, *War in Korea,* p. 60.

13. *Ibid.,* pp. 60–61.

14. Bruce Jacobs, *Soldiers: the Fighting Divisions of the Regular Army,* p. 211.

15. Colonel John Doody, interview-questionnaire, April 16, 1950; George B. Busch, *Duty: the Story of the 21st Infantry Regiment,* p. 21.

16. Roy E. Appleman, *South to the Naktong, North to the Yalu,* pp. 69–72, is excellent on the tank phase of the battle.

17. *Ibid.,* p. 71.

18. *St. Louis Post-Dispatch,* July 6, 1950, p. 1.

CHAPTER TWELVE

1. *Chicago Tribune,* July 7, 1950, p. 1.

2. Roy E. Appleman, *South to the Naktong, North to the Yalu,* p. 73.

3. *New York Times,* July 7, 1950, p. 2.

4. George B. Barth, "The First Days in Korea," *Army Combat Forces Journal,* II (March 1952), 23.

5. Twenty-first Regiment, "War Diary: July 5, 1950," National Archives; Headquarters, Twenty-fourth Division, General Orders, Number 51, 22 July, 1950 (hereinafter referred to as Number 51), p. 6.

6. Colonel Philip S. Day, letter to author, May 3, 1973.

7. Number 51, pp. 4–5. The clerk who wrote about this incident for the Twenty-fourth Division misplaced the action "near Chonan." Intrinsic evidence in the citation—such as the unit, the date, and other surrounding data—indicates it happened at Osan.

8. George B. Busch, *Duty: the Story of the 21st Infantry Regiment,* p. 22.

9. Appleman, *South to the Naktong,* p. 76.

10. Busch, *Duty*, p. 22.

11. Day, letter.

12. Number 51, pp. 8, 10.

13. *Ibid.*, p. 6; Appleman, *South to the Naktong*, p. 74.

14. Number 51, p. 4.

15. Busch, *Duty*, p. 22.

16. *New York Herald Tribune*, July 7, 1950, p. 1; *Chicago Tribune*, July 7, 1950, p. 1; *St. Louis Post-Dispatch*, July 7, 1950, p. 2A.

17. *Chicago Tribune*, July 7, 1950, p. 1.

18. Peter Kalischer, *San Francisco Chronicle*, July 10, 1950, p. 1.

19. Robert Leckie, *Conflict*, p. 71.

20. *Washington Post*, July 11, 1950, p. 1.

21. Number 51, p. 6; Appleman, *South to the Naktong*, pp. 75–76.

22. G-2, Twenty-fourth Division, PW Interrogations, July 6–July 22, 1950, National Archives.

23. *New York Herald Tribune*, July 12, 1950, p. 3.

24. Albert D. Biderman, *March to Calumny*; letter to author from Albert D. Biderman, November 14, 1972.

25. Appleman, *South to the Naktong*, p. 75, says two; Fifty-second Field Artillery Battalion, "War Diary: July 1–July 12, 1950," p. 3, National Archives, lists the three men.

26. *New York Times*, July 6, 1950, p. 3; Appleman, *South to the Naktong*, p. 75.

27. William F. Dean and William L. Worden, *General Dean's Story*, pp. 21–22. Barth, "The First Days," p. 23, states that Dean was there when Perry arrived, but neither the newspapers nor Marguerite Higgins, *War in Korea*, pp. 67–71, confirms this.

28. Higgins, *War in Korea*, pp. 67–68.

29. *Ibid.*, pp. 69–71; *New York Times*, July 6, 1950, p. 3.

30. *New York Times*, July 6, 1950, p. 1, notes that the North Korean radio announced 150 Americans killed in the battle and 50 others captured. Appleman, *South to the Naktong*, pp. 76–77, has somewhat better estimates.

31. Twenty-fourth Division, "War Diary: July 1–July 7, 1950," National Archives.

32. O. H. P. King, *Tail of the Paper Tiger*, pp. 187–188; *Chicago Tribune*, July 10, 1950, p. 2; Medical Section, Eighth Army, *Summary of Activities for Period 25 June–13 July, 1950*, "Army Reports," Truman Library.

33. King, *Paper Tiger*, pp. 186–87; Higgins, *War in Korea*, pp. 62–64.

CHAPTER THIRTEEN

1. Roy E. Appleman, *South to the Naktong, North to the Yalu*, p. 76.
2. Memorandum, July 8, 1950, George Elsey MSS, Truman Library.
3. Douglas MacArthur, *Reminiscences*, p. 332; U.S. Congress, Senate, Armed Services Committee and Foreign Relations Committee, *Military Situation in the Far East*, 82d Cong., 1st sess., 1951, p. 232.
4. Memorandum, August 9, 1950, Matthew B. Ridgway MSS, Carlisle Barracks.
5. *Time*, August 20, 1950, pp. 20–22.
6. Keyes Beech, *Tokyo and Points East*, pp. 140–41.
7. John E. Mueller, "Trends in Popular Support for the Wars in Korea and Vietnam," *American Political Science Review*, LXV (June 1971), 358–75.
8. *Ibid.*
9. *Newsweek's History of Our Time*, Vol. 2, p. 107.
10. James Thurber, *The Years with Ross*, p. 293.
11. "Princeton Seminars," p. 39, Dean Acheson MSS, Truman Library.

Bibliography of Materials Cited

MANUSCRIPT COLLECTIONS

Dean Acheson MSS. Truman Library, Independence, Mo.
ATIS Reports. MacArthur Library, Norfolk, Va.
Omar N. Bradley MSS. United States Military Academy Library, West Point, N.Y.
Eighth Army Records. Truman Library, Independence, Mo.
George Elsey MSS. Truman Library, Independence, Mo.
Fifty-second Field Artillery Battalion. "War Diary." National Archives, Washington, D.C.
G-2, Twenty-fourth Division. "PW Interrogations, July 6–July 22, 1950." National Archives, Washington, D.C.
Matthew B. Ridgway MSS. Carlisle Barracks, Carlisle, Pa.
"Special Collection." Historical Division, Department of State, Washington, D.C.
Twenty-first Regiment. "War Diary." National Archives, Washington, D.C.
Twenty-fourth Division. "War Diary." National Archives, Washington, D.C.
U.S. Department of State. "Memorandum[s] of Conversation," June 25 and June 26, 1950.
Arthur Vandenberg MSS. William L. Clements Library. University of Michigan, Ann Arbor, Mich.

ORAL HISTORY COLLECTIONS

Allen, George V. Princeton University Library, Princeton, N.J.
Allison, John M. Princeton University Library, Princeton, N.J.

BIBLIOGRAPHY OF MATERIALS CITED

Chang, John Myun. Princeton University Library, Princeton, N.J.
Sebald, William J. Princeton University Library, Princeton, N.J.
Vaughan, Harry. Truman Library, Independence, Mo.

PERSONAL CORRESPONDENCE OR INTERVIEWS

Albert D. Biderman
Carroll Blanchard
Philip S. Day
John Doody
George Elsey
Gabriel Kolko
Betty Boyers Mathews
Merle Miller
Glenn D. Paige
Dean Rusk
George Sam
Charles B. Smith
Kenneth R. Young

DOCUMENTS

American Military Government, National Economics Board. *South Ko-
rean Interim Government Activities*. Vol. XXXIV, July-August 1948.
Washington, D.C.: U.S. Government Printing Office, 1948.
U.S. Congress. *Congressional Record*. 81st Cong., 2d sess., 1950.
———, Senate, Armed Services Committee and Foreign Relations
Committee. *Military Situation in the Far East*. 5 vols. 82d Cong., 1st
sess., 1951.
———, Foreign Relations Committee. *Economic Assistance to China and
Korea: Hearings*. 81st Cong., 1st–2d sess., 1949–1950 (released
1974).
U.S. Department of State, Office of Public Affairs. *United States Policy
in the Korean Crisis*. Washington, D.C.: U.S. Government Printing
Office, 1950.

MAGAZINES

The Economist
Editor and Publisher
Life
Newsweek
Public Opinion Quarterly
Time

NEWSPAPERS

Chicago Tribune
Christian Science Monitor
Hartford Times
Los Angeles Times
New York Herald Tribune
New York Times
Pacific Stars and Stripes
St. Louis Post-Dispatch
San Francisco Chronicle
Washington Post
Washington Star

BOOKS AND ARTICLES

Acheson, Dean. *Present at the Creation.* New York: W. W. Norton & Co., 1969.

Allen, Frederick Lewis. *The Big Change.* New York: Harper & Bros., 1952.

Allen, Richard C. *Korea's Syngman Rhee: An Unauthorized Portrait.* Rutland, Vt.: Charles E. Tuttle Co., 1960.

Allison, John M. *Ambassador from the Prairie.* Boston: Houghton Mifflin Co., 1973.

Appleman, Roy E. *South to the Naktong, North to the Yalu.* Washington, D.C.: Department of the Army, 1961.

Baik Bong. *Kim Il Sung.* 3 vols. Tokyo: Miraisha, 1969–1970.

BIBLIOGRAPHY OF MATERIALS CITED

Barth, George B. "The First Days in Korea." *Army Combat Forces Journal,* II (March 1952), 21–24.

Bartlett, W., ed. *With the Australians in Korea.* Canberra: Australian War Memorial, 1954.

Beech, Keyes. *Tokyo and Points East.* Garden City, N.Y.: Doubleday & Co., 1954.

Biderman, Albert D. *March to Calumny.* New York: The Macmillan Co., 1963.

Bohlen, Charles E. *Witness to History, 1929–1969.* New York: W. W. Norton & Co., 1973.

Brumbaugh, T. A. *My Marks and Scars I Carry.* New York: Friendship Press, 1969.

Busch, George B. *Duty: the Story of the 21st Infantry Regiment.* Sendai, Japan: Hyappan Printing Co., 1953.

Caldwell, John C. *The Korea Story.* Chicago: Henry Regnery Co., 1952.

Caridi, Ronald J. "The G.O.P. and the Korean War." *Pacific Historical Review,* XXXVII (November 1968), 423–43.

———. *The Korean War and American Politics.* Philadelphia: University of Pennsylvania Press, 1968.

Collins, J. Lawton, *War in Peacetime.* Boston: Houghton Mifflin Co., 1969.

Daniels, Jonathan. *The Man of Independence.* Philadelphia: J. B. Lippincott Co., 1950.

Dean, William F., and Worden, William L. *General Dean's Story.* New York: The Viking Press, 1954.

Duncan, David Douglas. *This Is War!* New York: Harper & Bros., 1951.

Fields, Alonzo. *My 21 Years in the White House.* New York: Fawcett World Library (Crest Books), 1960.

Griffith, Robert. *The Politics of Fear.* Lexington: The University of Kentucky Press, 1970.

Gugeler, Russell A. *Combat Actions in Korea.* Washington, D.C.: United States Army, 1970.

Gunther, John. *The Riddle of MacArthur.* New York: Harper & Bros., 1951.

Gupta, Karunaker. "How Did the Korean War Begin?" *China Quarterly,* October-December 1972, pp. 699–716.

Halberstam, David. *The Best and the Brightest.* New York: Random House, 1972.

Higgins, Marguerite. *War in Korea.* Garden City, N.Y.: Doubleday & Co., 1951.

Jacobs, Bruce. *Soldiers: the Fighting Divisions of the Regular Army.* New York: W. W. Norton & Co., 1958.

Jensen, A. Kristian. *Internment, North Korea.* New Cumberland, Pa.: privately printed, 1953.

Jessup, Philip C. *The Birth of Nations.* New York: Columbia University Press, 1974.

Johnson, Lyndon Baines. *The Vantage Point.* New York: Holt, Rinehart & Winston, 1971.

King, O. H. P. *Tail of the Paper Tiger.* Caldwell, Idaho: The Caxton Printers, 1961.

Kinkead, Eugene. *In Every War But One.* New York: W. W. Norton & Co., 1959.

Kolko, Joyce and Gabriel. *The Limits of Power.* New York: Harper & Row, Publishers, 1972.

Koon Woo Nam. *The North Korean Communist Leadership, 1945–1965.* University, Alabama: The University of Alabama Press, 1974.

Kopke, Alan N. "The Beginnings of the Korean War." Unpublished manuscript, n.d.

Larrowe, Charles P. *Harry Bridges.* New York: Lawrence Hill & Co., 1972.

Leckie, Robert. *Conflict.* New York: G. P. Putnam's Sons, 1962.

Lee, Chong-sik. "Kim Il-song of North Korea." *Asian Survey,* VII (June 1967), 374–82.

Lie, Trygve. *In the Cause of Peace.* New York: The Macmillan Co., 1954.

MacArthur Douglas. *Reminiscences.* New York: McGraw-Hill Book Co., 1964.

McCune, George M. *Korea Today.* Cambridge: Harvard University Press, 1950.

Mathews, William R. *With Dulles in Korea and Japan.* Privately printed, 1967.

May, Ernest R. *"Lessons" of the Past.* New York: Oxford University Press, 1973.

Miller, Merle. *Plain Speaking.* New York: Berkley Publishing Co., 1973.

Mueller, John E. "Trends in Popular Support for the Wars in Korea and Vietnam." *American Political Science Review,* LXV (June 1971), 358–75.

Mullikan, Al. "The First Brutal Weeks in Korea." *Washington Post,* June 24, 1951.

Newsweek's History of Our Times. 3 vols. New York: Funk & Wagnalls Co., 1949–1951.

Noble, Harold Joyce. *Embassy at War.* Seattle: University of Washington Press, 1975.

Oliver, Robert T. *Syngman Rhee: The Man Behind the Myth.* New York: Dodd, Mead & Co., 1955.

Paige, Glenn D. *The Korean Decision.* New York: The Free Press, 1968.

Ridgway, Matthew B. *The Korean War.* Garden City, N.Y.: Doubleday & Co., 1967.

Sawyer, Robert K. *Military Advisers in Korea: KMAG in Peace and War.* Washington, D.C.: U.S. Government Printing Office, 1962.

Scalapino, Robert A., and Lee, Chong-sik. *Communism in Korea.* Berkeley and Los Angeles: University of California Press, 1972.

Schnabel, James F. *Policy and Direction: The First Year, The United States Army in the Korean War.* Washington, D.C.: United States Army, 1972.

Sebald, William J. *With MacArthur in Japan.* New York: W. W. Norton & Co., 1965.

Sheldon, Walt. *Hell or High Water.* New York: The Macmillan Co., 1968.

————. *The Honorable Conquerors.* New York: The Macmillan Co., 1965.

Simmons, Robert R. "The Korean Civil War," in *Without Parallel,* edited by Frank Baldwin. New York: Pantheon Books, 1974.

————. *The Strained Alliance: Peking, P'yongyang, Moscow and the Korean War.* New York: The Free Press, 1974.

Smith, Beverly. "Why We Went to War in Korea." *Saturday Evening Post,* November 10, 1951, pp. 22 ff.

The Statesman's Year-Book, 1950. New York: The Macmillan Co., 1950.

Stone, I. F. *The Hidden History of the Korean War.* New York: Monthly Review Press, 1952.

Suh, Dae-sook. *The Korean Communist Movement, 1918–1948.* Princeton, N.J.: Princeton University Press, 1968.

Symons, Julian. *Crime.* New York: Bonanza Books, 1966.

Thurber, James. *The Years with Ross.* New York: Grosset & Dunlap, 1959.

Truman, Harry S. *Memoirs.* Vol. 2, *Years of Trial and Hope.* New York: New American Library (Signet Books), 1956.

Truman, Margaret. *Souvenir*. New York: McGraw-Hill Book Co., 1956.

U.S. Army Infantry School. *Characteristics of Infantry Weapons*. Washington, D.C.: U.S. Government Printing Office, February 1966.

Warner, Albert L. "How the Korea Decision Was Made." *Harper's*, June 1951, pp. 99–106.

West, J. B. *Upstairs at the White House*. New York: Coward, McCann & Geoghegan, 1973.

Westerfield, Bradford H. *Foreign Policy and Party Politics*. New Haven: Yale University Press, 1955.

Whitney, Courtney. *MacArthur: His Rendezvous with Destiny*. New York: Alfred A. Knopf, 1956.

Index